CUT OPEN THE SKY

The Story of Connie Castro Jackson

Corliss Corazza
with
Connie Castro Jackson

Black Rose Writing | Texas

©2022 by Corliss Corazza
All rights reserved. No part of this book may be reproduced, stored in a retrieval system or transmitted in any form or by any means without the prior written permission of the publishers, except by a reviewer who may quote brief passages in a review to be printed in a newspaper, magazine or journal.

The author grants the final approval for this literary material.

First printing

Some names and identifying details may have been changed to protect the privacy of individuals.

ISBN: 978-1-68513-050-3
PUBLISHED BY BLACK ROSE WRITING
www.blackrosewriting.com

Printed in the United States of America
Suggested Retail Price (SRP) $19.95

Cut Open the Sky is printed in Sabon

*As a planet-friendly publisher, Black Rose Writing does its best to eliminate unnecessary waste to reduce paper usage and energy costs, while never compromising the reading experience. As a result, the final word count vs. page count may not meet common expectations.

For Ray Jackson

CUT OPEN THE SKY

INTRODUCTION

I met Connie Castro Jackson during dinner in an elegant conference room on the main floor of a large downtown Los Angeles hotel. Our husbands were good friends and both were there representing the transportation union that was hosting the event. They wanted to sit together, so the four of us squeezed into a crowded table. Barely past the pleasantries stage, Connie and I launched into a dialogue that took on a life of its own—we couldn't stop talking. We both understood that our meeting was no accident or coincidence, and thirty-five years later, the conversation continued.

I am extremely privileged to be the one chosen to put her story into book form. We spent many wonderful hours settled in her comfortable office while she talked through her experiences and shared her, at times, breathtaking wisdom. The stories rolled, and I recorded, prompted for more at the pauses, and asked for clarification and details. The hours flew.

Connie's information is down to earth, tinged with salty language—and a few adult scenes—and is loaded with insight. She says her work in this lifetime is to help people open up, find the lifeline to their innate wisdom and to tap into their own higher guidance. She helps people "remember, because we tend to forget" that a benevolent force guides us. This wisdom is in all of us, but the hard part is reaching it.

Her meditation classes have taught me that practicing meditation is a dependable and healthy way to navigate this crazy life. What snapped me awake to the depth of her wisdom and abilities was something she said during a reading. I was mourning the passing of my mother and felt raw with guilt over her having died alone. Connie had never met my mom, nor did she know the details of her passing. She quietly said she saw my mother (in spirit form) standing with me surrounded by bins of vegetables and fruit. Connie didn't understand the symbols at first, but I had picked up the urgent call from the hospital while I was in the produce aisle of a grocery store. Connie went on to say my mother knew I would feel guilt over having not been with her, so she came to me. This was precisely something Mom would do.

I've written this book in the first person, doing my best to capture Connie's voice, speech patterns, and inflections. This required considerably more than merely transcribing from audio tape—in fact, she has accused me of making her "sound smart," which, of course, she is, far beyond her own measure. I have purposefully kept myself and my own life out of her story. My part in her life and her part in mine, we will leave for another day.

Our goal in creating this book is to help you begin to see patterns, teachers, and lessons in your own life and to awaken changes in your perspective. Connie's stories cradle lessons, and they are free for the taking. We both agreed, if this book helps even a mere handful of people, our endeavor will have been worthwhile.

– Corliss Corazza

LESSONS START IN THE WOMB

I grew up on the dirt floors and in the fields of labor camps in the Central Valley of California. My mother's name was Josie Mills. She migrated from Oklahoma to California in 1935 with my five older half-siblings. She was a white-skinned blonde from Oklahoma who was escaping a bleak life with the alcoholic father of her first set of children during the worst environmental disaster of the twentieth century. The Dust Bowl. A combination of over-plowed land, drought, and sixty-mile-per-hour winds. People covered their windows, but dust continuously seeped in. They covered their mouths and noses but still choked. Crops were ruined, farms were lost, and job possibilities existed only in memory. People shoved what they could into whatever vehicle they owned, and ran for their lives.

During a lull in one of the waves of pounding dust storms, my mother's sister and brother-in-law came by her house to say goodbye. They had their old black pick-up loaded and were heading to a new life in California. My mother took a look at the man she had loved, who was a respected pastor by day, lying in his regular evening whiskey stupor. She felt the gloom of dust thickening the air inside and out and made the quick decision to pack up her five kids and the few items she could fit into what little room remained in her sister's truck. She left her husband behind, passed out cold. I don't know if she even wrote a note.

She was on her way to make a life picking crops in labor camps and would see her husband and father of her children only once again, years later.

My mother had married at fourteen years old and given birth to seven kids in Oklahoma. The twins died of diphtheria, and the remaining five moved to California with her. The San Joaquin Valley in the Sacramento region or Yuba City, further north, were rumored to offer the best opportunity for work. They chose the San Joaquin Valley.

Living in the camps was like living in a barn. Occasionally tents were provided or a building with one big room and sheets strung for partitions. No one had privacy, so workers became a big family. My oldest sister, Ruby, was a teenager with beautiful reddish-blond hair. I was later told by another older sister that Ruby could never adjust to the migrant worker lifestyle. She was used to Oklahoma. She was good-looking, very independent, and quickly caught the attention of men. One morning, my mother found an empty bed with a note on Ruby's pillow, saying, "Mom, I will always love you." She was seventeen, and she was gone.

Until the day she died, Mom cried over Ruby, wondering why she never tried to find us. For Christ sakes, we moved so many times, how the hell could she? She was fourteen years older than I, and surely dead by now, but I can't get a sense for how long. Not once have I felt spiritual energy coming from her. My half-brother Cecil, her full brother, became the fire chief in Isleton, California. Had she checked later in life likely Ruby could have found him.

When Mom, the kids, and my aunt and uncle finally arrived at the migrant workers' camp, the only people who would help them were the Filipinos. After meeting with a group of Filipino men, my mom said, "These are the strangest Indians I have ever seen!" The only brown people she had known were from the Cherokee

Reservation in Oklahoma. Mom and the rest were quite hungry, and the Filipinos took them in, fed the entire bunch and offered work. Mom met my father soon after her arrival. He was a Filipino farm worker named Ciriaco Castro, the sweetest man I have ever known. Barely five feet tall, dark-haired, with Asian features, kind, and gentle-natured, he must have seemed like a savior. Soon, she was pregnant with me, and I was born the next year, in 1937.

Five more kids, including me, were born to my mother in the camps, fathered by two different men. Every day we arose before the sun came up and were always sleepy and tired. We had no play time. By the time we were five, our job was to drag boxes out to our parents in the fields. It didn't matter how old you were, since babysitters didn't exist in our world. Every one of us went into the fields. In my earliest memory, I am younger than two years old, standing inside a wooden picking crate, crying for all I was worth. Just a fleeting memory, but it reminds me of how we were kept in place during the working day.

Mom loved all of us, took a no-nonsense attitude about raising us, and worked hard to take care of us. At a time when parents were giving up and sending their children to relatives because they couldn't feed or take care of them, my mother worked to exhaustion to keep ten kids fed and together as a family. She was too tired to be cuddly and warm, but we never starved or went without a roof over our heads, and all ten children survived into adulthood.

Of course, I didn't appreciate any of this until I was older, and now I wish I knew more about her. She lived her entire life of on the knife's edge of survival, which left no time for talking about the past or telling her stories. When she got older, we kids were busy with our own lives and didn't take time to listen when she finally wanted to talk about the past. I wish we had sat her down and videoed her stories. This is one of my deepest regrets. She was my first teacher, and I missed many of those lessons.

• • •

Prejudice was common in those days. The Mexicans and Filipinos kept to themselves. The farmers used this to their advantage. They would tell the Filipinos they were the good workers and Mexicans were lazy, so the Filipinos worked their asses off to live up to this reputation. It didn't help that Filipino self-esteem was flattened in the 1930s by the knowledge that, in some states, he or she could not own property nor marry a white person.

This story is old in the U.S. In the 1660s, Virginia became the first colony to prohibit interracial marriages. The thinking spread. In 1863, near the end of the Civil War, journalists trying to discredit the abolitionist movement suggested that freeing slaves would result in the interbreeding of "different racial types" with whites, diluting white superiority. These "different racial types" meant Blacks, Native Americans and "Orientals," which included Filipinos.

In 1948, the California Supreme court overturned its anti-miscegenation law—the first to do so. Nevada's law was repealed in 1959. Nonetheless, prejudice reigned. A Gallup poll in 1958 revealed that only 4% of American adults favored allowing interracial couples to marry.

I had no idea, in 1958, that it was still illegal in Nevada for my husband Ray and I to marry. At the county clerk's office in Minden, Nevada, we were told a white person couldn't marry an "Oriental." So, we went to Reno the next day, and I told them I was Mexican. Lucky for all of us, Mexicans weren't among the excluded "racial types." I didn't care. I had no birth certificate to prove it either way, so we were married and stayed married for nearly sixty years.

My mother and Ciriaco—or, Cherry, as he was called—were never married, and no forms of birth control were available. No safe or legal way existed for a migrant laborer to have an abortion, otherwise that might have been my fate. Mom spent the months while I was in the womb angry and frustrated. Embarrassed to be pregnant, she was even more ashamed to be carrying a dark baby. She never treated me differently from my white siblings, but I know. Her embarrassment passed to me through the womb. It became part of my makeup.

Years later, I would be reminded of my beginnings when my granddaughter Josie was born. She screamed when anyone picked her up except her parents. It broke my heart because she would wail and wail when I tried to hold her. During my daughter Deborah's pregnancy, she and her husband lived in a rather isolated situation and spent a good amount of their time talking to the baby. From the womb she was socialized to only those two people. Most of the time, fetuses are exposed to many voices. When Josie was born (named after my mother) the nurse was holding her and my son-in-law was talking on the other side of the room. This tiny, brand-new baby turned toward his voice. She recognized his voice, having become quite familiar with it while in the womb.

I didn't want to be dark-skinned. I could see: successful people were always white. I had gone into adulthood thinking that prosperous people were tall with light hair and fair skin. I did my best to wear hats and long sleeves and to stay in the shade. Years later, my teenage daughter Deborah, who I had always tried to keep as white as possible, was in our pool. I hollered at her to get out of the water and into the shade. In a rare fit of anger, she shouted back, "Goddammit Mom, if you want shade, get in the shade. I am sick and tired of you telling me to stay out of the sun." My feelings hurt and tears streaming, I went into the house and meditated into my inner self and asked why I was so obsessed with not wanting to be dark. That still, quiet voice within reminded me about the feelings coming toward me from when I was in the womb.

Now, I knew why I craved my mother's acknowledgment. She was spread thin with all those children, enough that finding the time to attend to just one was difficult if not impossible. I went after attention, bad or good. As a result, my mother and I were frequently angry with each other, resisting what we could have been learning from our relationship. Later in life, when Source showed me her anger came from not wanting me when I was in the womb—ah!—then I understood.

People live with issues from their time in the womb because we are blessed with no memory of events prior to our traumatic transit into the world. I can slap you now and you might become angry, but if you feel angry for no obvious reason, it might be that you are responding to a memory from before you were born. While doing readings in my practice as a Psychic Multilevel Channel, I have seen many issues resolved by helping my clients understand what happens to us while we are still inside our mothers.

By contrast I was a little star to my father, Cherry Castro. We had no television in the camps and very little entertainment. Dad would lift me on a table, give me what I thought was a microphone and tell me I was on the radio. I would sing at the top of my voice, a three-year-old superstar. The Filipino workers gathered around to toss me pennies and nickels. They loved it. I was a happy little kid, thanks to my father. I was his little darling. He called me "Consing." I'm not sure how to spell his sweet nickname for me, as it came with a little lilt in tone at the end.

Dad never raised his voice, never reprimanded me, and I always I felt his personality was much larger than he was. When I was about three, I wanted a ball and I wanted it *now*. Stores didn't stay open late back then, and we were driving through town after dinner. I remember little about my tantrum except that I was in the back seat and my father was driving. Mom was in front with him. He was completely bald, and I could see the back of his shiny head. And, oh boy, do I remember the conversation.

I hollered, "I want a ball!"

Softly, Dad said, "It's late and the stores are closed."

"I want a ball!!" I said, hollering a little louder.

My no-nonsense mother hissed, "Shut up and sit down."

"I want a ball! And I want a ball NOW! Damn you, you baldheaded bastard!" Imagine—I was three years old.

My mother snapped, "Backhand that child, Castro. Let her have it." Clearly, I must have learned those words from her, but that didn't stop her from wanting him to whack me.

Quietly, Dad said, "She just says that because she loves me."

Soon after, my father went away, but I didn't know why. I contracted polio around the same time. I remember my mother telling me to get out of bed, but I couldn't move. "Get out of that Goddamn bed!" she yelled.

"But I can't move!" I said.

She didn't believe me because I was a kid who needed much attention, meaning she thought I was looking for attention, again. The next thing I knew, I was in a hospital, in isolation. I was three years old. I thought my family had abandoned me. In those days, they didn't treat babies as beings with feelings. Most of my fears started then, I think. I began calling the nurses Mama. They were all "Mama" to me. I don't know how long I was hospitalized, but I remember that one side of my body was paralyzed and twisted. I ended up in braces.

One day, my dad came to the hospital with a tricycle and said that if I would walk for him, I could have the tricycle. He was good for his word, and I eventually got the trike. I guess the hospital was two-story because as my condition improved, the nurses would hold me up to the window to see my family down below waving at me. I don't have much recall of this time because my family never talked about it, and I never asked questions. I do recognize that this was my introduction to abandonment.

I still don't know what happened between my parents, but I know it didn't take long for my dad to be replaced by my monster of a stepfather.

EXPERIENCES ARE LESSONS

Late summer in Courtland, California, meant the air was thick with Sacramento River Valley heat. Five or six of us kids were still at home. My oldest sister Ruby had long since run off. One brother had married and moved on, as had my sister Ruth, with a husband and child. Two older brothers, plus a handful of youngers, lived with us. We were a mix of ages and heredity. I was in first grade, and I had started seeing spirits.

My mother had rented a rambling old rundown farmhouse near the railroad tracks for the upcoming winter, with a wide porch and plenty of space. Spirits walked in and out. I heard voices and footsteps in rooms that were unoccupied. Whether I heard them or not, always I felt their presence. One day Mom was in the kitchen at the far end of the house cooking rice, beans, and vegetables with meat, she called chop suey, which was one of our staples. We kids were enjoying a rare day at home, and I was playing on the porch in the shade, when I heard my mother call, "Connie, I said lunch is ready NOW!" It must not have been the first call because she sounded pissed.

I stood, in the slow way that meant I was in control of when I actually did go inside, and started across the porch, stopping short when I saw a group of people. At first, I thought it was our family with my grandmother. They were sitting at a long, wooden table under a tree in the yard by the barn. We had no phone, so in those days, seventy or so years ago, family and friends dropped by without notice. As they were dressed like Grandma, who had moved out to California from Oklahoma, and looked very elderly, I almost hollered, "Grandma!" But I froze and dropped to the floor behind the railing. I didn't know these people. Plus, I could see through them! They were almost solid but mostly transparent. They were there and yet they weren't.

I found a little knothole in the porch railing through which I could watch them. The two women were dressed to the ankles in drab housedresses, and the man had on a long, black, dusty coat and a hat. He was petting a beautiful gold and white collie dog who dutifully sat at his side. The man took puffs from a pipe. I could see smoke curl from the bowl. The group laughed, or appeared to laugh, happy to be together, just like any family. The man was alternately slapping his knee and petting the dog, but I couldn't hear them. It was like watching a silent movie. I wore a second- or third-hand thin cotton dress and, mindless of the rough wood and what it was doing to my knees, I crawled fast as I could along the porch to the kitchen; keeping low so the transparent family wouldn't spot me. I was six years old and terrified.

When I crawled into the kitchen, late for lunch, I was in trouble. I pointed and used my loudest stage whisper, "There are some strange people out in the yard." My brothers and sisters jumped up from the table and ran to the window to see.

Of course, they saw no one, which added to my troubles! My Pentecostal, no nonsense mother bellowed, "What are you doing? Get up, get in here, and eat *now*!" I had the reputation of needing extra attention and my mother did not have time or patience for me.

My sister and I slept on the couch in the living room, and one night, as we lay in the quiet, I told her about the footsteps and voices. Then—I was a little shit—when I was sure she was scared enough, I quietly said, "They're going to get you."

She rocketed under the covers in complete terror as a strange voice quietly said in my ear, "I'm going to get YOU!"

Now I was screaming, and I jumped on my sister, and the chaos began. I never expected ghosts might have a sense of fairness.

That house scared me. I felt them, and I could sense them and see them. The spirits were transparent people, walking around. I had the sense that they lived there and mostly weren't aware of us. Sometimes I heard a child's playful voice. I find it interesting that I could hear the child's voice but not the adults. Either way, I never talked to these apparitions—God no. Just the opposite: I was petrified.

My sister and I had to go upstairs to clean the top floor where my brothers lived. The women did the house chores then, but we were only five and six years old. We went up the stairs hugging each other, taking one slow step at a time. My sister felt a presence, too, stronger in the upstairs. At night, we could hear people walking up there when the brothers weren't home.

My mother paid no mind to any of this. She said it was "just my imagination" or me looking for attention yet again. I would say, "Mom, those strange people are here," and she would shoo me off, saying "Get outside and go play."

What she didn't know was that on my way to school was a sunflower patch. One sunflower stood taller than the rest, and I swear it watched me. As I walked to the bus it turned very slowly, as if to follow my movement. I walked past it, at a crawl, then when I got up close, I ran and looked back. It was facing me! Now, was this my imagination, or was the whole damned place haunted?

I didn't know then, but this was my first taste of what was to be a very interesting life.

• • •

My dad was psychic, although he didn't understand or realize it. He used to tell people he could read palms. He held a person's hand and looked at the palm and told them about their life. He was receiving information psychically, but he didn't know it. Palm reading was familiar to him, so it made sense for him to give a reading while holding up a palm, and he was quite accurate. When he met my husband Ray, Dad called me to the side and said "How come he can only have girl babies?" I will never forget that because we never mentioned that Ray had two daughters. Later on, Ray and I had a third girl of our own—our daughter Deborah.

Ray loved my dad. If Dad needed money, Ray was there for him. Everybody who met him loved him. He was fun and loveable, always the life of the party. Barely clearing five feet tall, his features looked Chinese, his hair was dark, and his equally dark eyes were full of kindness, sparkling with a touch of mischief. Because of his bigger-than-life personality, when we planned a party, friends asked if my dad would be there. He loved to be the center of attention, and when he danced, other dancers stepped aside to watch him. His first language was Tagalog, but he knew a bit of Spanish and English. He loved to sing, sometimes mixing languages, confusing everybody, but no one cared. Instead, they sang along.

Dad was very nice to Ray from the moment they first met. They had to work to bridge the language barrier for their friendly talks. I didn't know it at the time, but my dad had reservations about my choice of husband. One day he quietly said to me, "Why don't you like brown men?" I saw then that prejudice runs deeply and on both sides of the street. That shocked me. I was my dad's little darling. His Consing. I did not stop to think he might feel unsettled about his little Consing not marrying a brown man.

Still, he was proud and excited when Ray and I bought a house. He had come to the United States as a laborer, and during that time the Anti-Alien Land Law of 1937 was enacted, banning Filipinos from owning land in the U.S. The law was ruled unconstitutional in 1941. The injustice stayed with him even though it didn't affect him directly. A fieldworker's wage never would have been enough to buy property or even in most cases allow workers to afford rent. But here I was, his little Consing, married to a white man and living in a house we owned! A house with a toilet! He was over the moon. We wanted him to feel like it was his house too, so he had his own key. One night, Ray and I were sitting up in bed reading. At about nine o'clock, we heard the front door open and my dad talking. He was giving a tour of the house! "This is my daughter's front room. This is my daughter's kitchen. This is my daughter's toilet," and so on. By then Ray and I were cracking up, and here Dad comes around the corner, right into our bedroom, with three other guys. "This is my daughter, and this is her husband, Ray." They all nodded politely, and we heard the lock click on the front door as they left. Ray and I were belly laughing by then.

Today, Dad might be diagnosed with obsessive-compulsive disorder. When he came to our house and parked in front, it took him a good twenty minutes to come inside. He got out of the car and walked around to the passenger side, checked it over, ran the window up and down and locked the door. Then, back to the driver's side to check the lock, back again to the other side to check that lock again. Not done yet, he checked each tire, carefully, and, finally, the trunk. Only then did he come to the front door. Meanwhile, Ray and I stood at the window timing him and giggling.

As far as I know, my dad never married until he was older. He certainly never married my mom, a white woman, as it would have been illegal. Interestingly, my mother hated my father, but I have never known why. I wish I had asked. I also never knew why he left us when I was little. Probably for the same reason. Although they both lived in Stockton, there was no getting together. As the years went on, however, he always had a woman. They came and went, and I was never close to any of them, until Ba Bing. She was with him until he died and was good to him—the sweetest person ever. She came from the Philippines to visit her sister and somehow met my dad. Her English wasn't very good, and since they lived more than an hour away, we kids didn't see much of them, but when we did, I was surprised to see my dad being a little tyrant with her. I think it was the first time he felt he had any power, but she was sweet and good to him and didn't deserve it. I'd get after him for being bossy and tell him to stop. He would say, "Okay Consing," and then stop. Anything I said to him was okay because I was still the apple of his eye.

• • •

My mother did her best to keep us in school, but sometimes this was possible only after harvest. This meant that we went to school in early November; but only if our job was close enough for us to walk to a school. In some cases, a one-room school house that served the farmer's kids might be nearby, and we got to attend, too. Migrant kids were told to sit together as a group. Lessons for grades kindergarten through eight were taught, but we were usually so far behind that we were taught as a group. We moved with the harvest three or four times per year, never catching up.

I will never forget when we moved to Lathrop, forty-five minutes south of Courtland and an hour south of Sacramento, and bought a house. My mother worked, begged, and borrowed to afford the friggin' down payment, but we got a house! The guy selling it was a great big Texan with a booming voice and a bigger line of bullshit. The house had a kitchen and two bedrooms. Every place we had ever lived had an outhouse, but this one came with indoor plumbing.

Oh, Jesus Christ, we had a house! Our address was on Schilling Street. When picking season started, we usually moved into tents near the field and then moved to a rental house when the work was done. A few years back, I could still see the trees that border the field in Brentwood where we picked fruit. A factory now sits where there used to be cutting sheds. We also cut fruit for drying while we lived in the tents. Buying the Lathrop house meant we had a home to go to during the off season for a couple of years.

Then one day, Mom said, "We have to move."

She didn't own it after all, and the big Texan hadn't owned it either. The rightful owner took over and displaced all the people who lived in the neighborhood: we weren't the only ones scammed. People like us never fought for rights, as we didn't have money for lawyers.

I drove by one day decades later to show my husband Ray, but, as you might guess, all kinds of new houses sit there now, and we couldn't find the street.

Life went back to the way it was. Tomatoes and peaches were picked and onions topped. We weren't supposed to but we ate some as we worked. The men cut asparagus, in a stooped position all day long. No restrooms. You had to find a place to go outside. The heat was horrible. We wore hats and tried to keep covered as much as possible. Nothing existed to make the working lives of these people easier until Caesar Chavez took it upon himself to fight for the rights of farm workers, but conditions remained bad. It is still back-breaking work. When I hear people complain about their jobs, I want to tell them to try working in the fields all day, and then they will be thankful for their soft chairs and desk jobs in air-conditioned buildings.

At fourteen I went to work in the cutting sheds. We cut fruit to be dried—apricots and peaches. At least I was in the shade—if the shed had a roof. At sixteen I went to work in the canneries making thirty-five cents an hour. I thought I had made it big, but to this day I still can't stand the sickening smell of hot tomatoes or hot peaches. Imagine: "making it big" meant long hours on my feet, night or day, with few breaks.

I worked in the sheds until I got my hairdressing license. Beauty school was hard, but I was determined. I watched my mother go without sick leave, telling people that she didn't have time to get sick. She would take a week off to have a baby and then get right back to the fields, bringing the baby with her.

My English was so bad, it was impossible to learn well no matter how much time I spent in school. My education was spotty, as I've said. My mother had an Okie "twang" and very poor English, and my father had his Filipino twist on English. I knew nothing about my dad's family in the Philippines. Nor did I learn their language because I didn't want to be dark-skinned, as the prejudice against dark-skinned people prevailed. Now I am sorry I didn't learn Tagalog. I understood it as a child because I was around it all the time, but I never had learned to speak it.

Tagalog was not the language of success and wealth.

Even then I wanted to fit in with successful white people. I didn't want to know about my mother's past, either, because she was poor, and that was not the life for me. So, I hid, afraid people saw that I was poor, not white, and not smart. Fear of people finding out the truth about me emerged as panic attacks years later. White meant family, having a house, having a telephone in the house and a toilet. Everybody I knew was brown, except my mother, and they didn't have any of these things. I thought to be happy you had to be white, and yet there were lots of happy times when I was little in the migrant camps.

ANGELS, TEACHERS, AND GUIDES

I've told you that teachers come into our lives to guide us along our spiritual path—teachers who don't necessarily know they are teaching us but happen to be in the right place at the right time, saying or doing the right thing. The person who causes you to feel is your teacher. We learn to handle frustration, fear, anger, and to seek peace, happiness, joy, and love from our fellow humans across the years of our lives. You can see why I say we are all teachers for each other.

Lessons can come at us from a positive direction or a negative one, and we are on our own to determine what is to be learned. I might overhear someone mention a book or class or film that turns out to be exactly what I need at exactly the right time to move me forward on my path: that person is a guide. Or, a man might give me an appreciative look on a day when my self-worth is bottomed out: he is an angel. Angels show up on our paths when we need kindness. They are the people who stop to help us on the road when our car breaks down, etc. They help in whatever way teaches us the most. At times angels use fear when we need to learn difficult lessons fast. As we become aware that we are surrounded by teachers, guides, and angels, we begin to see the massive spiritual choreography afoot.

My first glimpse of the psychic world came through the pest control man. I was twenty-two and had no idea what a psychic was. He came to spray and immediately started talking about a dream he'd had. Why in the world was this man talking to me about his dreams?

I don't remember what we discussed, but he said, "You sound like a psychic."

I said, "What's that?"

Shrugging his shoulders, he said "I don't know, but I have a book at home that reads like you talk."

The subject of the book was Edgar Cayce, and the concept of a psychic sounded crazy to me. A few weeks after that, one of the girls at work said, "There is a guy in town. He just moved here, and he is starting some classes. They sound interesting, They're psychic classes. Connie, you might want to go." This was not a coincidence but guidance pushing me in a direction.

Soon, I heard of more classes and more books, and my journey had begun.

• • •

When I was six years old, I knew I wanted to become a hairdresser. My family had no money for school, not then, nor ever. No obvious way existed for me to achieve my goal, and yet I lived through my girlhood with that dream and plan. In high school, to my surprise, a classmate told me about a vocational program run by the school district. Suddenly, beauty school was free. That classmate was my guide.

Stop and think quietly about teachers, guides, and angels who have supported you along the way. I urge you to think about this and list them, along with details of what each has done for you. Valuable perspective can be gained from looking back at the help you have received.

Direct guidance brought me to my husband Ray. I needed to see my father and my car was broke down. My friend, Marilu, volunteered to give me a ride. She knew a shortcut by the railroad and knew the railroad crew on duty. As we pulled over, she honked and waved. They smiled and waved back.

I said, "Wow I'd like to meet him, the guy on the left."

The two ambled over, happy to see Marilu. The young man on the left introduced himself as Ray. I had called over my future husband. No coincidence, and no, we've never looked back. From the first moment, I loved that tall, handsome man with the ruddy face, eyes deep with intelligence that sparked with humor and, as I would learn, darkened in anger.

• • •

My first psychic teacher was a man named Bob.

In the 1960s, I went to classes where Bob was teaching psychometry, which is a form of extra-sensory perception characterized by the ability to sense vibration from an object while holding it. In the vibration are details the holder senses about the owner's life or the object's history. I am a perfectionist. If I can't do something perfectly, I don't want to do it. On this night, I was holding Bob's keys, trying to understand what I was supposed to do. I felt lost and told him that I wasn't getting it.

Bob said, "You'll get it. Close your eyes and see me in your imagination." I was in a class of twenty people and all were at attention.

He added, "Just watch me in your imagination."

I saw him, and he was kissing another guy!

Bob asked what I saw, and I told him.

He turned bright red and quietly said, "You are psychic."

After class I asked him what the image I saw was about.

He told me I had seen him kissing his boyfriend.

"Oh, you're one of those," I said. Remember, this was the sixties and gayness was not discussed. Gay people stayed firmly in the closet. Early on Ray had taken me to Finocchio's, a very popular, world-famous club in San Francisco, which from 1936-

1999 showcased female impersonators. Only then did I learn that people can be gay.

I never asked, but I am sure my future husband Ray must have gotten a kick out of my naive amazement.

As it turned out, Bob was a perfect first psychic teacher for me. Sadly, he died of AIDS several years ago, and I will never forget him.

Bob was the real thing, but I met my share of fakes.

One Saturday I went to a séance. I had been going to every class or lecture I could find. Just couldn't learn enough fast enough. I was excited to go. Bob was hosting and a medium was supposed to be present.

When the séance was about to start, the speaker/medium, who was dressed as a minister, got up and ushered us into a dark room. The windows were blacked out, and the setup felt authentic. I sat in front so I wouldn't miss a thing. Shapes were visible, but nothing could be identified. Voices called out the names of loved ones who had passed over, but I knew the speaker was a fake by the way he treated a beautiful black woman, who was a professor at the University of the Pacific in Stockton, as we had learned while waiting for the evening to begin. She was beautiful, articulate, and intelligent. A shadowy figure emerged from the back of the room and began to sing: *"Mammy's little baby loves shortnin' shortnin', Mammy's little baby loves shortnin' bread."*

I couldn't believe it, and felt terrible for her. I thought, "Oh my God, this is a scam." Racism gave him away, at least to me, as he reduced the woman's loved ones to a stereotype. When we arrived, he had told us to fill out a card telling him who we were and who we wanted to talk to. He had a good reason to ask this—to later prove how psychic he was—but he had taken those cards on stage with him. Rather than being psychic, he was merely a good reader. His helper made a big deal out of blindfolding him, so he "couldn't see." He would grab a card and know the content spiritually, then give his answer. Bob later said that he realized the guy could see under the blindfold and was reading the cards. People were furious, but I wasn't. I thought it was good entertainment and a lesson in itself.

I have met many good people and a few crazy ones. For example, I was invited to a group of UFO people dressed in foil and little peaked hats who said they were aliens from the Mother Ship. Now, come on, before you judge me, remember in those days I was open to everything. Actually, I was quite excited to meet an alien. Although, the fact that people were buying into this irritated me. I found it amazing and sad that people so strongly want to believe in something that they will fall for the most ridiculous imitations.

During this time, I was still living in Stockton and didn't recognize that I was being introduced to spiritual education. I was judgmental and ignored much. In a meditation group I was a part of, a girl started coming who talked about guides and guidance, and she talked about things I'd never heard of. I thought she was too "out there," and I was probably rude to her. I might have even rolled my eyes. Now, I realize she was coming in as guide for me, but I judged her, so I couldn't hear it—I wasn't ready. On our path we get "whispers." As I look back, I realize she had much to share. The Universe can't give to us until we are open to receiving.

• • •

Becoming a hairdresser also was no accident or coincidence. One skill was the perfect launch pad for the other. During this time, Bob stopped teaching because this kind of teaching was deemed illegal. Devil worship, possession, and related subjects were against the law. One night he called, saying he had been arrested. A sting was set up where six policewomen were sent to him for readings. He was warning me in case I was contacted for information. He recorded his readings and because of similarities between the readings, he was deemed a charlatan. In truth readings can be similar because we overlap: we humans share certain characteristics. Bob was quite talented as a psychic, but he was arrested for defrauding the public. He was given a fine, but thankfully no jail time. His minister's license was sufficient to get him released—go figure!

A church in Modesto called The Universal Life Church would license you to perform marriages. I hold such a license. Don't ask me to hold church meetings or stand up and preach, but I can marry you and your sweetie.

Thousands of people are ministers of ULC. I once performed a wedding on the coast of California at a beautiful venue on a promontory overlooking the ocean. The bride, groom, and their guests faced the refreshing view, while I took in the back of the hotel and the hotel rooms' verandas. A naked couple enjoying the sun on chaise lounges were positioned about one floor up, right in my line of sight. The man, who was standing to watch the nuptials, shifted and alternated his feet on the railing, causing his "equipment" to lob right or left. He must have been giving the woman an account of the action below, because occasionally she sat up and took a look. Hell, I could hardly perform the ceremony.

When I started beauty school at sixteen, I was one of only two-dark skinned girls. Because I hadn't finished high school and my vocabulary was so low, I felt intimidated by my classmates. The teacher was the biggest white woman I had ever seen, and she scared me to death. Learning was hard because I was scared. She drew me aside one day to tell me I was close to flunking out. I "couldn't get" the theory. Much of the time I felt too afraid to pay attention to what she was trying to teach us. However, my practical work was perfect. She said the only reason she was keeping me in school was because of how good my practical work was.

Then one day a Japanese woman became my teacher. Mrs. Kio was brown and small like me. She did not intimidate me. Instead, she adored me, taking me under her wing.

I had no money and only one uniform. One day, I was riding to school with a girlfriend when we had a flat tire. No choice but to fix it, and by the time we got to school, I had grease on my one and only uniform. The teacher I was afraid of sent me home to change. At that time, I still lived with my family in Lathrop, which took two busses to get to and two to return. With the time it took to get the grease out of my uniform, I was gone a good part of the day. Soon after Mrs. Kio gave me a second uniform, an extra one she said she never wore.

In 1957, just before I was to graduate with my beautician's license, Mrs. Kio came to me and said, "Connie I have a job for you in the best salon in town. I don't want you to get started in a cut-rate shop, because if you do you will get stuck there."

Never will I forget what she said next: "I want you to come by my house so I can make sure you look good and are dressed right before you go to your interview." Adding, "Jo French is rough. She is scary rough, but it is the best shop in town, and you will learn so much from her. I have your salary set. You are going to make forty-five dollars per week and don't let her talk you down because this is set. If she says anything less than forty-five, you tell her Mrs. Kio said forty-five."

On the day of my interview I followed orders and went to Mrs. Kio's house. She dressed me, fixed my hair and got me looking good. I was terrified, knowing this was my way out of the field and the life of a migrant worker. Eighteen years old and scared to the point that I could hardly walk. I opened the shop door to its owner, Jo French, cussing out a worker so loudly I couldn't breathe. She sat me down and barked, "Kio said you were the top student in the class and that's the only reason I am even talking to you." Then she snapped, "I'm going to try you out for two weeks and your salary is thirty-five dollars per week." I never said a word to correct her.

I always have felt that Mrs. Kio's purpose in my life was to move me along in a direction I did not know—could not have known—existed. An angel, guide, and teacher all in one. Sadly, she died right after I got that first hairdressing job.

And I did get that job.

I am five feet and one inch tall, and Jo French was six feet tall, white-skinned, and had the foulest mouth I had ever heard. She wore a white uniform, reddish-brown pin curl waves, blue eyes, and spoke in a megaphone voice. She was as crude as she was loud. I can't describe how terrified of her I was. Plus, she never used my real name. Instead, she called me Fart.

I was dating Ray by then. When he called the shop, she would answer and then announce, "Hey little Fart, Big Prick's on the phone."

In those days, women came dressed in their best to get their hair done. They wore skirts and hosiery, never pants, talked about their charity work and luncheons. This was even more so the case at Jo's shop, which was high-class all the way.

At some point early on, Jo asked me to dial "time." I was too afraid to tell her that I didn't know what that meant. In those days, apparently, you could dial a certain number to learn the correct time, which people did when they forgot to wind their watches. I never had even used a telephone. Labor camps didn't have phones, and when we "owned" the house in Lathrop, we couldn't afford one. I had to work to keep myself from crying.

One of the other girls realized my problem and dialed the number for me. I felt deeply grateful. I learned later that on a rotary phone, you only had to dial the letters POPCORN and a recorded voice would tell the time.

Adding to my shroud of poverty was the fact that I had an old car. It was some kind of a cute Ford, blue with blue taillights. I loved those taillights and didn't know they were illegal until I was stopped one night.

The officer said, "Did you know you have blue taillights?"

With a big grin I said, "Yeah aren't they great!"

"Maybe, if they were legal."

He checked the horn and the windshield wipers, and they didn't work either. He decided not to check the brakes, figuring, I presumed, that they didn't work either.

"You know what? If you will have all of these fixed by next Tuesday, I won't issue you a ticket. You have enough problems." I guess he noticed, too, that the doors were tied shut with ropes.

I parked blocks from the shopping center in Stockton where Jo had her shop, because I didn't want anyone to see my car and know how poor I was.

Working was not cheap. I had to pay for gas, lunch, and uniforms. I quickly realized I couldn't afford to work. My entire body did not hold enough nerves to tell Jo I had to quit. I stood in the back room ready to cry, when she walked in. Without looking her in the face, I said, "I have to quit."

She shot out, "WHAT?"

"Jo, I can't afford the gas to drive here."

"What do you mean?" she bellowed.

"I have to make car payments, dentist payments, and give money to my mom, and I just can't afford the gas to work here," I said to her shoes.

Softly, Jo said, "Meet me at Bank of America in Stockton at 1:00 p.m. on Monday."

Despite having no idea why, I met her in a glossy bank building where she asked me to list everything I owed, then proceeded to take me to each of my creditors, paying them in full. Next, she had me open a bank account and showed me how to use it. Jo knew every one of the bank's employees.

She said, "Now, I want you to put money in your account, I don't want it to be hard on you. When you have saved up enough, you can pay me back. I don't care how long it takes."

Before I could find my voice, she said, "How much is your car insurance?"

I didn't have any.

She screamed at me, "You don't have insurance?"

I didn't even know what insurance was, except that it was in no way part of the life of a migrant worker.

Later, Jo called up her insurance agent and set me up with the first insurance I ever had or had ever heard of. This beautiful woman, Jo French, my huge, crude angel, came to my rescue.

Another time, Jo told everyone in the shop they needed to have their own scissors, thinning shears, and bobby pins. Boy, was that too much for me to afford. I was spending my lunch hours at a dress shop two doors down from the beauty shop because I couldn't afford lunch and didn't want anyone to know. I loved a red velvet dress that hung in that shop. It fit like a glove. I went over every day to try it on and pretend. I couldn't afford it, but I could dream. Then came the day the dress was gone.

My dress was gone.

Christmas came and I opened a box from Jo. In it was my red dress. I couldn't believe it. Not only the dress, but silver shoes and a silver purse to go with it. She also gave me scissors.

I whooped, "My dress, my dress! How did you know?"

Jo replied, "Connie, I would have to be blind and stupid not to know."

The girl who owned the dress shop was Jo's friend, and she had said, "Would you please buy this dress for that kid? She is wearing it out trying it on."

Even still, Jo was hard to work for. She would say "Hey Fart, mix up a half of brown and a half of red."

When I came back out with the color, she told me to put it on her client's head, critiquing my work as I went along, while she worked on another client right next to me. When she leaned over to say, "Now why did you do it that way?"

I had to explain in front of the clients, which embarrassed me.

She would say, "Now, why did you do that color? Why did you mix that?"

I would say, "I don't know, Jo."

And she would say, "Are you stupid?"

But she was teaching me about color. And it worked. At my next job, I worked as a colorist. Jo French, a hardcore teacher, taught me to do one of the toughest jobs in hairdressing without my realizing she was doing it.

On another day I came into the shop, and she stood between me and the appointment book. I always tried to avoid her, but she was against a wall, and then her husband came in, putting me between the two very tall giants.

To my surprise, they started to fight—physically fight. She grabbed him by the shirt with her arm across my neck. Stuck between them with a wall to one side, the pressure was choking me. I didn't say a word, as I was raised to keep my mouth shut. She pulled forcefully at him, choking me, cussing a blue streak, with me now hanging by her arms. Still, she didn't let go. I think I was blue by the time she was done.

The thought came to me that I needed to move on.

I was offered a job in another shop, so I took it.

Weeks later, I ran into Jo's husband. He said, "Oh my God, Connie, Jo hasn't stopped crying since you left."

"What do you mean? She hated me!"

"She didn't hate you. She loved you."

"But she treated me like she hated me."

"You know, Jo loved you because she saw herself in you. Her parents were alcoholics, poor and tough with her. She is gruff but very loving. Her way is all she knows because that is what she has been taught."

It was no coincidence that I ran into Jo's husband. I needed to hear her story.

He said, "You were like a daughter to her. Look at how she treats me, and I love her." It was true. Jo regularly cussed him out in front of everybody when he came into the shop.

I never regretted moving on, but I do regret never acknowledging her kindness. I many times thought of sending her a note but never got to it. Then, I heard she died. She and Mrs.

Kio, two important teachers, both gone. A huge lesson not to put things off, to acknowledge those who deserve it while we can.

• • •

Before I met Ray, I was in beauty school among all of these beautiful white people but without a boyfriend. The girls chattered on about their dates, while once more, I didn't fit in.

One day one of the girls at the shop said her boyfriend was coming home and bringing a friend, did I want to meet him?

I said, "Oh God no!" I was so shy she might as well have told me to murder the guy.

Well, I met him anyway, and wow was he good looking. His name was Art Reed, and he was tall, white, blue-eyed and handsome.

And, here is the thing—he instantly fell madly in love with me. Just when I was feeling out of place, unworldly, uneducated, and unloved, here comes this fabulous guy to love me. I was flattered.

Art was in the Navy, and this was during the Korean War. His family was in Glendale, and he was stationed nearby. He came to see me every weekend, but we knew he was going to be sent overseas soon. We arranged for me to take the bus so his family could meet me. He met me at the station, at about 1:00 a.m., then we took another long bus ride to his family's beautiful home. He took my hand, walking me to the back of the house. A beautiful swimming pool shimmered, lights reflecting in the water. I felt like Cinderella as he knelt and gave me a ring.

In my shock, I only said, "Does your family know I am Filipino?"

He replied that he didn't think he had mentioned it, but he loved me so they would too.

I wasn't so sure.

I was seventeen years old and had never eaten steak or used utensils or sat in a nice restaurant. Art's parents wanted to take us for a steak dinner. Oh God. We went to what I thought was a night club. Dark and dramatic inside, the people sparkled, as they sat around tables with crisp white cloths and a battalion of forks, knives, and spoons on either side of the plate. What the hell were they all for?

When time came to order, I looked at the menu, sweating when I badly wanted to look classy. I didn't want to order anything too cheap because Art and his family might think I was cheap, and yet not too expensive because, well, I didn't want to appear to take advantage of their generosity. I had all this stuff going through my mind, trying to fake it.

I saw Phillip Mungo on the menu and thought, well, I'll order that.

"I'll have the Phillip Mungo please," I said.

The waiter said, "Huh?"

Art came to my rescue and said, "I think she wants filet mignon."

Then the waiter asked if I wanted it medium or rare, and I thought, "When is this ever going to end?"

But it continued, "What would I like for salad dressing?" Good God, we never had dressing at my house!

Art came to my rescue and ordered for me, but I will never forget the most embarrassing dinner of my young life. His family were kind, acting like nothing happened. They threw an engagement party for us. Art had a sister who had several young friends who came to the party.

All were white and gorgeous and crazy for my Art.

I wondered, why did he choose me?

One day I went back into the bedroom I was sharing with Art's twin sister. The door was cracked open and his mother and a neighbor, who thought I had gone out, were talking, I heard every word.

The neighbor asked, "What do you think of her?"

"Oh, he'll get over it." His mother said.

"Doesn't it bother you that she isn't white?"

"I have learned that if I just go along with him, it will all just blow over."

I sat and cried. I never told Art what I had overheard, but I thought, "Ah, I knew they wouldn't like me." I have to say that the whole time I was there, they treated me like a princess.

Interesting the Universe put me in the right place at the right time to hear that conversation.

Still, we were madly in love and planning to marry when he came home from overseas.

He was stationed in Japan and had been there a few months when I got a "Dear Jane" letter, telling me he was shacking up with a Japanese girl in Japan. The letter was beautiful, and I appreciated the effort, but my heart was broken.

During the eighteen months he was in Japan, I completed beauty school and became licensed as a hairdresser. I decided to become a blond. When a Filipino woman starts to bleach her hair, the first stage is orange. More embarrassment. On his way home from Japan, Art came for a visit. I walked in the door with this friggin' orange hair while he sat there looking at me, a little in shock. My little sister had been telling him all about Ray, this great guy I was dating. Sweet guy that Art was, he said the most wonderful thing: "I understand you are pretty serious. He must be a terrific guy or you wouldn't have chosen him."

That was the last time I saw Art. He was central to a very sweet time in my life. Having him come along when I so badly needed confidence gave me the confidence to complete beauty school and the courage and freedom to fall in love with my Ray

JUDGMENT

A young and exuberant Donald Caruso blew into my shop in Stockton on a wintry day. We started swapping stories and were soon to become great friends. He was a college student in his early twenties, and I was at least a decade older. His soft brown curls and lively eyes made him attractive; but what really caught me was his energy—that of a warm and loving person. Our friendship expanded from the beauty shop to my living room. He loved to visit with me, although he wasn't interested in learning about anything spiritual at first. But, finally, he asked to have his Tarot cards read. Looking back, I could see he was testing the waters with no expectation of the flood that was on its way. I think he could sense my sensitivity to spiritualism and on a deeper level knew he needed to become enlightened.

I believe we are here to be who we are and to allow others to be who they are, as we all grow and learn. If only we could see that negative judgment is in the eye of the beholder, who is in position to learn from their own lessons. At the same time, we teach what we need to learn. As quoted by many people "The one with the problem is the one with the problem." For instance, if you think your friend, husband, or coworker is too sensitive or pushy or loud—take a look at yourself. Is it you who are one or more of these things? People become frozen in fear of judgment when they are judgmental themselves.

If I had decided to judge Donald Caruso as too weird, I would have missed the experiences of a lifetime. Donald was hearing an unfamiliar voice and it was making him behave in ways that terrified him.

By the spring of 1980, Ray and I had married and moved to Benicia, California, leaving Stockton behind. I had severed most of those relationships, didn't call or visit, but a couple of years later, Donald rushed through the doors of the beauty salon where I was working in Benicia saying, "Oh my God, I have been looking and looking for you!"

I asked, "What's wrong?"

"I just need to talk to you."

I met him at my house after work and said, "Donald, if you are going to tell me you're gay, I have known that since I met you."

He started to cry, I think with relief, admitted he had tried to commit suicide. He had gone through much sorrow because in his Portuguese, Catholic, old country background, homosexuality was not accepted. Neither was it accepted in the United States at the time, as a rule. Since I last saw him in Stockton, he had completed his education and was working as a school teacher. His school's principal came with him that day. Donald wanted the man to meet me. I don't think the principal was prepared for what he witnessed. I wasn't either.

We settled in with coffee, Donald and his boss on the couch. Since we last met in Stockton, Donald had married a sweet girl named Nancy who did not suspect he was gay.

He said, "Connie, something really strange has been happening to me. This is why I want to talk to you. I might be going crazy. A voice keeps coming through my thoughts and is talking to me. I don't know what this is, but it isn't pretty." Then, looking away he said, "Nancy told me never to do this in the house again."

"Uh, do what?"

"I go into a trance and my tongue wags," he looked down.

"Your tongue wags!" I gasped. Oh shit.

"Well, let me see what's going on."

Without warning, he started to jerk. He jerked so hard, he knocked a big picture off the wall before falling to the floor, flopping like a fish out of water. Then, a voice—*not his*—came out of his mouth. And so did his tongue. I swear to God, I have never seen a tongue that long. It was hanging out of his mouth. I thought, "Oh Jesus, this is a possession. Anyone would think this is a possession."

Getting hold of myself I said, "Who are you?"

From Donald's mouth came a much slower, lower voice, "My name is Hombre."

Well shit, I thought, great name for an entity possessing a married, gay, Portuguese suicidal Catholic.

I said again, "Who are you?"

He started to answer but was hard to understand because Donald was jerking violently with this huge tongue hanging out.

"Why is Donald having such a hard time?"

Hombre replied, "He is having a hard time accessing my energy."

To check his authenticity, I asked a personal (to me) question, one that Donald had no way of knowing.

The answer I got from Hombre was the truth and pure as gold.

I asked Hombre to step aside so I could talk to my friend. Donald opened his eyes, shivered, and complained he was freezing. I grabbed a blanket, covered him, and said, "Donald, we have to talk. You never want to do that in front of anybody. They will put you in a looney bin. You are channeling a consciousness named Hombre. If you want to do this and you want to start letting Hombre in, we will have to start working on your energy so you can access it easily."

He and I worked together until he learned how to channel the energy of Hombre, and I set him up in circles of people I knew would appreciate it. At that time, in addition to my salon job, I was traveling all over doing classes on spirituality. I asked Donald to come along and he did. His switch was on when he was around people. He was engaging, entertaining, and everyone loved him. Once a month, the same people gathered and Donald held his circle. He'd strengthened his energy so that his tongue no longer wagged, the shaking subsided, and he jerked only once when Hombre took over and once when he left.

Right away people began to ask questions. Hombre went around the circle answering and giving information. He was accurate to the point that at times I worried Donald would be run out of town. Remember, this was still the 1980s and tolerance for spiritualism was low. People who valued his ability were fascinated that a channeled spirit could recite details about their thoughts, relationships, and lives.

As long as he was accessing Hombre's energy, Donald was fabulous. Obvious maybe only to me, he changed back to himself the moment Hombre departed. At that point Donald retired to the bedroom to nap, then got up and started again. His sessions often ran into evening.

Once, a cute young girl asked questions. She appeared happy until Hombre said, "Your marriage is just about over, and you will be getting a divorce this year," at which she broke into tears. Hombre was decent enough not to mention the affair in front of the group, and later the girl confided in me that she already knew her husband was having an affair.

Another time Ray and I were talking to Hombre, and he said, "Ray, you will be selling this house." It was the first house we owned in Benicia. At the time we had no intention of moving, and I thought, *Well, he missed that one*, but sure enough, the opportunity to buy our next house showed up, and we did sell and move.

Even considering the support of many ardent followers, Donald was not happy. He loved being a schoolteacher but wasn't attached to doing Hombre. The presence of other people energized him, but he felt depressed when he was alone. His energies were misaligned. On the one hand, his father was strict, old-world, and unprepared to understand homosexuality. On the other hand, Donald had been raised with sisters and a mother who loved him, had a sweet wife, and eventually two beautiful kids. On yet another hand, he felt miserable and embarrassed living a lie. His one desire in life was to be loved by a man.

None of his life's pieces fit together, yet Donald was all about love. At my insistence, he told his wife that he was gay, and they later separated. "It is unfair for her not to know," I said.

Donald taught me not only that we need to spend time and show love for the people in our lives, but he opened my eyes to reserving judgment. He had friends who were unique beyond my experience—interesting, shall we say. One day Donald said, "Connie if you ever want to give a workshop on a larger scale, I have a friend with a huge ranch. The house has a second story that is one big room. It would be perfect for a big group, and my friend said I could use it any time." I thought he was excited to plan an event for me, but an odd brightness in his eyes caught my attention—a twinkle.

I set up the workshop for forty of us. We arrived at a beautiful farm house. I won't tell you the location. You'll see why. As we drove up, I noticed a shed housing a restored buggy, jaw-dropping in its detail, with a yoke for horses. Beautifully groomed matched teams of horses grazed across the acreage from a sparkling swimming pool and manicured landscaping, all of it gorgeous and inviting.

"Where will forty of us be able to sleep?" Keep in mind that we'd been asked to bring our own bedding.

"The second floor of the house is large enough," Donald said. He took me inside, and I felt him watching my face. The door swung open to a black leather swing, hanging from the ceiling. On another wall hung an expensive-looking black leather whip, and in a far corner sat a massage table with strap restraints.

I was thinking, *What the hell is this?*

Next, I saw a life-sized toy lamb with a hole in the rear end, and in another corner, a full-sized horse with a black leather saddle. Donald, who had been having a great time watching my face, broke out laughing.

"What the hell is all this? Where have you brought me?"

I was not laughing.

"Connie," he gasped, trying to catch his breath, "my friend is one of the top dominatrices in the United States. This room is for conventions. People come from across the U.S. to attend."

Donald admitted that she had offered to put stuff away, but that he had told her not to. "I want my friend Connie to see this!" he told her. He enjoyed his joke several times as workshop attendees showed up.

As it turns out, Donald was the lookout for the most unconventional of "conventions." This high-powered dominatrix had befriended him. (I never really wanted to know how they met.). She had married a wealthy farmer who died, and she didn't want to run the ranch, so she lived in the city and hired people to keep the place going, showing up only for her monthly conventions. An average-looking woman, she was easy to talk to and happy to explain ranch activities to me. The beautiful buggy was for her guests. They pulled it, four at a time, as though they were horses, while she whipped their asses with a whip. Inside, teams of mostly straight men dressed in bow ties and leather pants waxed her floors on their hands and knees. Again, she whipped. This form of entertainment was quite illegal at the time, unexpected and completely unacceptable in farm country in the early 1980s—for Christ's sake!

I asked the woman whether any of this was about a sex act, and she said, "No, people would be amazed to know that these are doctors, lawyers, and congressmen."

She never named names, but said her clients were intelligent to the point where they were not balanced emotionally. Used to giving orders and being in charge, they'd forgotten how to feel. To generate sexual excitement, they needed to be subservient. When she whipped their asses and ordered them around, they found the balance they needed. Again, she said, sex was not involved. I often wondered about that.

The dominatrix didn't share all of her secrets, but neither did I know what questions to ask. I had never heard of a dominatrix. This was quite an education for me.

I was giving a class in meditation, weeks after this experience, and Donald called to ask if he could bring three friends.

"Of course," I said.

When they arrived, it came to me that something was really different about these people. During the lunch break, one woman walked over and in a deep baritone rolled out, "Nice to meet you, Connie. You and I are in the same business."

"What business is that?" I couldn't imagine.

She said she sort of did counseling.

After the class, Donald was laughing hard, loving l the fact that I was shocked. Through unstoppable laughter he choked out that the person I had just talked to was a dominatrix and popular enough that she was on a magazine cover that month. He showed me the magazine and there she was in a little black leather bikini holding a big black whip. First of all, I could hardly imagine a magazine of this sort existed let alone now have three of these women in my class. These turned out to be fun, great people. What an excellent lesson about judgment.

• • •

Life is always clearer in hindsight, and many times I've wished I could go back and spend precious time with friends who have passed, to let them know how much I care. Donald is one of those people

On a Monday, he called to say, "Connie I have to talk to you."

No time, I told him at first, but then I found a way to work him into my schedule. When he arrived, I was finishing a reading for another client, suggesting to Donald that he go lie down and take a short nap, and that I'd be freed up shortly.

I'll never forget the look in his eyes when I asked him what was wrong.

"I don't want to be here anymore," he said softly.

After I finished the reading, I went in to wake him, but he said he had to leave. He had to see his kids. He swept by me and out the door.

Donald Caruso left my house on Monday and was found dead on Tuesday. Imagine my regret. When he hadn't shown up for work, teacher friends went to his house and found him dead on the bed with his earphones still playing music. Despite an autopsy, no cause of death could be determined.

I have thought about this often. Is it possible to wish yourself gone?

Relationships, with me but also with other friends, had given him relief from his dread of being judged, but in the end it wasn't enough.

• • •

While I learned much from each of these experiences and losses, Ray Jackson turned out to be the most significant teacher and strongest supporter in my life. From the beginning, he backed me up on everything I did, even all the craziness I went through when I was educating myself about the psychic experiences I was having, including people like Donald. For the most part, he cast no judgment. Whatever I wanted to do was fine by him and any money I wanted to spend was always available.

I flitted from one class or gathering to another—a free soul—and yet I was afraid to go to events out of town alone. Ray never judged me for that, nor did he try to stop me from going—in fact, he drove me where I wanted to go. While I attended the gathering, he kept himself busy checking out the town, having a meal, or settling into a place to read. He never complained or expected me to miss anything I wanted to attend.

One night, Ray was at work on swing shift, four to midnight. I was sitting in our front yard with neighbors who had heard UFO's were supposed to be visible in the sky that night. We were sitting on lawn chairs, looking up, when Ray pulled in.

He sauntered in and asked, "What's going on?"

I said we were looking for UFO's.

He kept going saying, "Okay see you later."

Ray may have been laughing on the inside, but he never showed it. He never embarrassed me or made me feel less than. Occasionally, he would privately tease me and call my practices "Woo-woo." But years later, I heard him talking to a friend saying, "You know, I never had a belief in this stuff that Connie does, but over the years I have seen her do some amazing things."

Money was not important to Ray. If we had enough, we had enough. He donated money, loaned money, and gave money away. He unconsciously practiced non-judgment, the lesson most of us fail time and time again. I fell in love with him one evening in 1956. The third time we had been together, he was at my house where I lived with my mother. Mom took me aside to say she was out of money, couldn't buy groceries, and didn't know where to turn. She asked if I thought Ray might lend her money. She was that desperate. I was embarrassed to ask him. Later in the evening I drummed up the courage, and he immediately opened his wallet. He had just cashed his paycheck and had the money divided into two sections—one amount for child support and the other for bills. He pulled money from the bill section, since he never would short his little girls, and handed it to me without hesitation.

When we had been married a few years, one night we were dressed up for a night out and headed to a Mexican restaurant in downtown Stockton to meet some of the railroad guys Ray worked with. He was young—they all were young, fun to be with—but a pecking order was in place, and those with the most seniority had the right to harass the new guys. The younger men did their share of ribbing also, which was more along the lines of camaraderie and not meant to be mean—they just had a lack of awareness. I learned that night that they had let up on teasing Ray about my dark skin, but nothing stopped them from their prejudice against people with black skin. Outside the door of the restaurant was a black man asking for money. Ray stopped and asked if he was hungry. The man said he sure was, so Ray invited him to join us. We walked right in. Ray made sure he was seated between us and told him to order anything he wanted. I wish I remembered the guy's name. He was delightful and entertained us with his stories and had us laughing and joining in.

As we were leaving, I saw Ray quietly hand him a wad of bills before we walked out the door. Remember, this was the early 1960s and most people would never do this.

Ray never mentioned this until years later, but since he was married to a brown-skinned woman, he was a target, and for years fielded comments like, "Eating rice again tonight, Ray?" He never said if the ribbing got any uglier, but I got the idea. Still, he loved working for the railroad and when he retired, he loved equally working for the United Transportation Union and supporting railroad employees.

Now, I don't want to paint the picture of a perfect person, Ray could be a compete asshole. He had his Scorpio temper and absolutely hated it if I challenged him on anything. He would holler and storm out the door whenever we got into it. I remember a fight where he said I thought I was always right and at the same time I was hollering the exact same thing about him. It could have been funny if we weren't so pissed off. But wow, the people I've met, and I owe it to Ray, who never judged me and who was always willing to take me to places I was afraid to go to alone.

Before that, however, when I was sixteen and the time came for me to start taking my beauty school courses, we were so desperately poor that I thought I had better start right away, rather than put it off another year until after I graduated night school. I finished my junior year and started beauty classes. This means that I do not have a high school diploma, which has been a real stickler with me. I didn't have the label or the paper, but neither have I ever needed it.

In light of that, imagine this:

I was asked to conduct a workshop in Belvedere, a ritzy area of California. Fifteen women were scheduled to attend. The woman who had hired me called the morning of the workshop and asked, "Connie I need to ask you, what are your credentials?"

I told her that I wasn't sure I understood what she was asking.

"Most of the women attending today are PhD's, and I wanted to warn you ahead of time that they will probably ask you what your credentials are."

"Carol, the only thing I can say is that my credentials come from the highest level."

She thought that was a good answer. Where do you get credentials for being what you are? Who certifies you as a spiritual being? This is how accustomed people are to using labels to define our identity.

Another friend of mine, Alona, was obviously a Democrat. You couldn't see her car for the labels. Make Peace, Not War. Gratitude. Think Globally; Act Locally. Plastered to her car was virtually every bumper sticker motto in existence. One day she said she was sick and tired of her daughter being label-conscious. She even took a Macy's bag with her when she shopped. If she bought items at Penney's or Sears, she carried them out of the store in the Macy's bag. She didn't want to feel embarrassed when people judged her for shopping at less-exclusive stores.

Alona went on and on. "I am just sick of her being so label conscious!"

"Alona, have you seen your car?"

Clearly shocked, she said, "What are you talking about?"

"Well, take a look at your car. Aren't you also trying to tell people who you are? You have the need to have all of those labels on your car. Isn't your daughter doing the same thing?"

She called me when she got home, "You aren't going to believe this. My daughter took all of the stickers and labels off my car." Alona and I were talking about labels, while her daughter was driving home the point by removing them. Coincidence? I don't think so.

Labels give us identity. When I don't know who I am, I examine my labels. By the time we are born, or even before, we have been told who we are. We are not perfect; we don't do things right: Do it my way. My way is the right way. Don't touch it you'll break it. Be quiet. Don't move. Not that way! Be careful! And on it goes. The truth is that we are spiritual beings. We are made of love and compassion—that's the core of us. When we are hungry, we cry so someone will feed us. We learn to trust in this way. But we are told that satisfying our hunger is not enough. We must *achieve*. In order to achieve we must smell a certain way, have a certain education, the right body type, the right clothing. We become programmed not to express ourselves, but to please society, the group. Imagine, a sweet little energy coming into this life not consciously knowing who or what it is. Then, based on the input it receives, it begins to reprogram itself—like a computer. Others put information into the little computer, which it gathers because it doesn't know it doesn't have to, nor does it know how things work otherwise.

People start as pure energy. We're not about skin. Skin is just a container. We come into this earth so we can learn to find our way. The Universe throws us roadblocks and curveballs until we do—although some people never find their way. At some point we have to go back and get in touch with that original energy. We have to remember ourselves before programming. I always tell people if they want to read a truly spiritual book, read the *Wizard of Oz*, written by L. Frank Baum. Dorothy is trying to get home. She gets to a place she doesn't know, she has no identity, and she is trying to find her way home. The Scarecrow, Tin Man, and the Lion are her guides. She has to climb a mountain and fight off those little devil things and kill a wicked witch. Of course, she is actually fighting her inner battle to remember who she truly is. She thinks she is fighting with external forces trying to prevent her from reaching the Emerald City, only to learn that she is the one who is wise, she is the one with strength. The knowing lay within herself, where it always had been, just like she always had been home, and was from the start.

We walk through life thinking that if we just perform correctly, everybody is going to love us. We don't realize that our whole journey is about learning to love.

Reaching the point where we can live without judgment or the fear of judgment has a learning curve like anything else, and it is relative to our backgrounds. The most difficult people to reach are the ones who don't share. In order to connect with others, we have to share ourselves because it opens up our energy field. So, suppose now I am sharing who I am and that means I am perfect and wonderful because as long as I was hiding who I am, I was admitting that I was not perfect nor wonderful. Sharing is hard to do because of the fear of judgment.

I had a woman—let's call her Jill—come in for a reading, and she was so worried she couldn't sleep. She had been told by a psychic that her daughter would die a painful death.

Then, her daughter called a few days later and said, "Mom, I need to make out a will."

Oh my God, that's when Jill called me, terrified. She thought her daughter now knew that she was soon to die.

I said, "No, your daughter didn't know that—you sent her that signal."

You see, we send signals without saying a word. You might verbalize your support of a friend's actions or decisions, but if you are harboring inner thoughts of disappointment or disapproval, that person hears it spiritually. It's a signal he or she can detect. Our thoughts are most important because that is where all is created. Our whole chakra system is connected to our thoughts. Meanwhile, the body-mind connection also works together. When I am doing a reading and the client is telling me about a loved one they are concerned about, I am in that loved one's energy. How do I get into their energy? Through my thought. I can look at a person and think, "George, what is going on?" and George will talk to me in my thought. When a person worries about George, they are talking to him. This is why so often you can be thinking about a friend or family member and the phone will ring, and it will be them. The object of worry can't heal until the worrier heals and stops judgment. Jill herself, convinced of the truth of what was actually bogus information about her daughter's death, worried hard enough that she passed the idea on to her daughter. We want to be careful not to manifest our worries.

Peace comes when you let go of judgment and/or expectation. The person you are judging or having expectations of needs to become more important than your expectation. This is how we abolish prejudice—by abolishing judgment and letting go of expectations. That person needs a chance to prove themselves, to appear in your line of focus exactly as they are, not what you want them to be. You must remain in love. When you set expectations as more important than the actual person, they feel it as rejection. If you are suffering from judgment or expectation of yourself, meditate. Open yourself to Source and ask what you are supposed to learn. Know that when you judge, you deck your energy. A good goal is to meditate daily and talk to your inner self to come up with the answers. You don't need to ask anyone else your question. If you practice meditation and are able to tune out all but your inner voice, the answer will come to you as a thought or idea. This is Source. Be open to receiving it. The information you receive is about yourself. Understand that a power greater than us exists, that we are both human *and* spiritual beings. The human side holds frailties: jealousy, hate, fear, judgment. The spiritual side is love and compassion. Through meditation, ask for wisdom and for help connecting human and spirit.

Of course, like anything else, you get better with practice.

When I was still a girl in school in Lathrop, maybe second or third grade, I had a friend, Beatrice. One day we were in the bathroom, and Beatrice said, "Connie can I see your tail?"

I said, "I don't have a tail."

"Yes, you do! My mom says all Filipinos have tails!"

"Well, I don't think so, but we'll look."

I pulled my pants down, and I spread 'em.

She said, "I don't see a tail."

A popular derogatory term for a Filipino at the time was monkey. Don't ever call a Filipino a monkey or you will have a fight on your hands.

That evening I said to Mom, "How come I don't have a tail?"

I felt pissed not to have a tail.

She turned slowly and quietly said, "What are you talking about?"

"Well," I rattled on, "Beatrice said that Filipinos have tails. Her mom told her."

My mother, carefully and in dead silence, got up from the table and with me in hand marched to that woman's house.

She slammed her fist into their door, calling Beatrice's mother out. "How dare you tell my daughter that she has a tail!"

She was loud, cussing and beating on the door for what seemed like an eternity. Beatrice's mother was apparently smart, however—smart enough to stay inside—and we finally headed home.

I had lost my little friend. Beatrice was never allowed to see me again. This was new for her, but not for me. Often other kids were not allowed to play with us. Prejudice is the ugliest, most short-sighted form of judgment.

• • •

I mentioned earlier that my stepfather was cruel. Cruelty is also a form of judgment. In the camps we were raised never to ask questions or cause trouble. At an early age I knew to keep my mouth shut and keep the peace. That was the way of the migrant camp. If you were in pain you didn't complain. If you saw something you shouldn't have, you didn't tell. You certainly did not cry—emotions meant nothing, but survival did. So, this man came into our lives, became my stepfather. And he was mean. He was also so possessive he wouldn't let us see our own father. The only way I could see my dad was if we were working in the same fields.

One time I saw him and ran to him, and he said, "You have to go back, don't stay here."

"But I want to see you," I said.

"You can't stay here. I don't want you to get in trouble."

Dad knew the man was mean, in fact everyone who worked with our stepfather knew it. I saw him cut a guy with an asparagus knife. They were gambling, and he caught the guy cheating. Those knives were razor sharp. I remember lots of blood and lots of screaming. My mother grabbed us out of there quickly. I don't think I ever saw the cheating man again, but we might have decided to move to another job. The camps were closed societies. Nobody ever called the police. People took care of their own problems—quietly.

The Filipino were so close-mouthed that if you asked, "Do you know so and so?" they would say no, whether they knew the person or not.

I remember I went down to skid row, where the Filipino men hung out waiting for work, and asked a man, "Do you know Ciriaco Castro?"

The man pretended to think for a minute and said, "No." The next week I found the camp where my dad was, located him, and that same guy was sitting right next to him. They closed ranks and protected each other. It was very hard to ever find anybody, which might help to explain why my half-sister Ruby never found us.

Our stepfather hunted us down. My one full sister is a year younger than I. Having friends in the house was difficult, and really, we didn't want to bring anyone home because we never knew what mood he would be in. He never talked. He just said, "Get out."

I always called him "Asshole" under my breath. I never called him Dad.

One day a little friend of mine came to the door, and I heard this voice say, "Hello Mr. Asshole. Is Connie home?"

Thank God Mr. Asshole didn't understand English all that well.

Not only did we rarely have friends over, he was so jealous and possessive that he wouldn't let us go anywhere, either. My sister and I went to a wrestling match one day. We used to love wrestling matches. My mother said we could go, but Asshole must have pried our destination out of her. We saw him walking up the walk to the Civic Auditorium in Stockton and knew we were done for. Our fear of him was so huge, we stood up and followed him out without question. My mom had four more children by him, and I don't remember him being mean to his blood kids, but they may tell the story differently. The rest of us got the strap, and those of us not being striped at that moment had no choice but to listen to the one who was. I don't know that it happened very often because we were so terrified of him, we didn't dare commit the crimes that were guaranteed to put us in that position.

Later on, when I was eighteen and working in the salon, my mom qualified for some kind of government aid for the first time. "Mom," I told her, "We don't need him anymore. Get rid of him." All of us kids were present when she in no uncertain terms told him he couldn't live there anymore and that "they" would put him in jail if he didn't leave. Filipinos in general were easily intimidated by the thought of jail and the people in power who might put them there. Apparently, our stepfather was, too, because he immediately packed and left.

You know, everybody gets theirs, eventually. Talk about Karma. When he died, he was pretty much alone.

I never talked to my mother about how bad he was. We were all protective of her. I would see her sitting in the mucky mud harvesting celery, pulling up that damn celery. I wanted to help her in whatever small way I could, and when I was little, I had an idea to help her by washing the clothes. I filled the tub with bleach—straight bleach. I put in her underwear and any other pieces I could find. We didn't have much in the way of clothes, but I grabbed what I found and dropped it in the tub, then rinsed each piece and hung it on the line.

Two days later we were in the car and Mom said, "What is wrong? Something is going down my legs."

When we got to where we were going, she got out and saw that the fabric of her underpants had pulled away from the elastic and was disintegrating into little pieces, slithering down her legs. "What the hell!" She couldn't believe her eyes. My conscience made me fess up to having done the wash. Boy, did I get in trouble for that. She had a hard time seeing the good intentions of a little kid when her underpants were sliding down her legs.

My mother loved us kids in her own way. She raised eleven of us, having lost twins to diphtheria in Oklahoma, but she was never taught how to be affectionate. She exhausted herself making sure we survived. If anyone were to say or do anything negative to her kids, she would fight them like a banty chicken. Mom taught us that love is more than hugs and words. We show love in the way we have been taught. Learning how to show love has been a huge lesson in my life. She outwardly loved my daughter Deborah, however. I always felt that she was loving me through Deborah. She showed the affectionate love to her grandkids that she couldn't show to us because she had been too damned tired.

The result of all of this is that I have searched most of my life for acceptance. I had to be taught rejection in order to recognize acceptance when it came. The resistance we feel—guilt, jealousy, fear, prejudice, and more—is set up in us early in life when the platforms from which we learn are built. In relationships, each time I reached a point where I felt rejected, and I lived in fear of being alone. We must experience the impact of these emotions in order to understand them and grow.

On the positive side, raised in migrant camps with people who had nothing, but still shared what they did have, I learned that poverty has its joys. Nobody went without food, and I would not have developed the compassionate nature I have today if I had not learned it as a child. Both sides of me were being fed, human and spiritual. As a six-year-old kid in the fields, I dragged a bottle of water around to see if anyone wanted a drink. I felt so sorry for them working in the heat. That set the pace of my life, and I continue to hold compassion for people who have nothing. I understand what loss and lack is because I lived it and felt it.

My belief is that by the time we are five or six years old, our lessons have begun in earnest. Who we are, combined with our life's experiences, equals spiritual growth. Having a mean stepfather is no accident or coincidence: he taught me the concept of fear—and how to face it. My real father taught me unconditional love and loss, and my mother taught me that there are many ways to show love. Looking back, I understand that when I started seeing ghosts and spirits at the age of six, I was being set up to recognize the value in my ability to channel and use my inner sight later on.

None of us would be the people we are today without our human experiences.

• • •

Years later, there I was, set up with feelings of fear and abandonment and married to my husband Ray. At times I wonder whether he would he have taken the bait and said "I do" if he had known what he was getting into. One day, after we were married, I remember crying because I felt rejected and unloved by him. Then, I heard my inner voice say, "When are you going to learn he is your mother and father?" Meaning, he plays the same roles, teaching me the same lessons about needing acknowledgement, fear of abandonment, and rejection. Obviously, I hadn't understood those lessons yet; and so, they had to be repeated.

I realize I have a problem with abandonment and rejection and that it is *my* problem, no one else's. I can work on it within myself, and I don't have to make you like me. Whatever our issues are, we will always find them sitting on our path. As we learn to handle them, we will see the same lessons less and less and be bothered by them less and less. For instance, years ago, if you and I were having a conversation and you said you didn't like my clothes, I would have passed judgment on the situation, taken it into myself as an insult, deeply and personally, feeling completely rejected and disliked. Now that my perception has shifted, I can realize that it is just about the clothes and personal taste and that you have a right to your opinion. Before I shifted and understood this, I didn't feel peaceful. If you feel resistance to a person or a situation—in effect *judging* the situation, you are inside a lesson. If resistance diminishes and you begin to feel peaceful, you are learning the lesson.

A good example of my judgment causing resistance has to do with Ray's first wife. I wanted to think of myself as the better mother, so of course she had to be the evil one. In my mind, I was the superior person, and I stubbornly refused to try to understand her. Looking back, I can see where much of her pain came from, but I couldn't then. I couldn't see where much of mine came from either. She didn't want to share her daughters with me or Ray, but I didn't want to share with them with her either. Instead I judged, resisted learning, and I didn't feel peace around her and her position in Ray's life until I recognized the situation as a lesson. We see the other person as the bad guy, but that person is holding a mirror to us.

We were living in a house in Stockton, California, and I was sitting in a chair in our living room at about seven in the evening. Ray worked for the railroad and didn't get off his shift until eleven, and I was alone. Suddenly, I heard a loud scraping noise in the family room, which scared me to death. I listened to the noise and thought, *Oh God, did I lock all the doors?* Frozen with fear, I then heard a loud *crash! bang!* I sat, completely terrified in that chair until Ray got home. My purse and keys were in the kitchen on the table, and since the family room and kitchen joined, to get my keys and escape I would need to pass through the frightening family room. I could not make myself move, no way.

When Ray found me, I whispered "Something has happened in the family room."

Leaning backward he said, "I'm not going in there."

We crept in together to see a wooden, carved tiki head lying on top of a ceramic elephant I had gotten in Mexico. But how in the world was it on top of the elephant when they had been at opposite ends of the room? The tiki head, which we had picked up at a flea market, had to have flipped to end up face down on the elephant. We couldn't make sense of it.

I called Bob, who was my psychic teacher at the time, and told him that the tiki head had crushed my elephant. It was in pieces and the tiki head didn't have a mark on it.

"Well," he said, "it's quite obvious your tiki head didn't like your elephant."

Smart Ass. But he did explain that certain cultures believe that when someone dies, their souls can be absorbed by objects and that strange things can happen with objects from other countries. The belief system of origin would stick with the item and might not be aligned with the belief system in its new home. It makes me understand how personal reality is.

Years later, in that same house, my granddaughter started talking with a Southern accent. She and her mother, Mary, had come to visit, and the little girl sat on the hearth next to that tiki head. Shauna began to speak, not to us, but to someone in the room visible only to her. She was talking on and on with an accent and gesturing with her hands.

Astonished, I said, "Shauna where did you learn to talk like that?"

She innocently said, "Like what Grandma?" She didn't even know she was doing it, and I was immediately sorry I hadn't kept my mouth shut so that I could have listened longer.

I got rid of that damned tiki head.

But what was it that happened? Did a kind of energy enter her body? Could energy have breadth? Was it because of who I am and my reality? Did I create this experience so I could learn about my own power?

Another time our friend Dean saw a blonde in a bathrobe floating through the house. Dean came to visit frequently. He worked with Ray and attended union meetings in our home. The view down our hallway was visible from the kitchen. During the meeting, Dean saw a white woman with blonde hair in a pink bathrobe. She was looking at a picture on the wall, and then she softly turned and continued down the hall.

After the meeting, Dean asked, "Who is your friend?" I told him no woman was there.

He said, "I saw a woman in a pink bathrobe!"

He was certain of what he had seen, and he was pissed. He knew he had seen a woman and thought I was lying to him. He did not believe in "any of this psychic stuff." We went together and looked all through the house; in closets, under beds, behind curtains—everywhere. I never saw her again but other strange things happened in this house. Floors creaked and doors slammed shut or open with no one near them. Ray dismissed my claims of hearing the doors slam, but one night we were in bed and the front door opened and then slammed closed. I knew what it was, but just to show him, I asked Ray to check and see if it was our daughter Deborah coming home. He got up and checked. When he came back into our room, he had the strangest look on his face when he said, "She isn't home yet."

Two doors down from me lived a woman who I had become friendly with. She was not into anything psychic that I know of. We had never discussed it. She came over one day and said that there was something strange going on at her house. She said, "I keep hearing a baby crying for its mother. I can't find the baby, and it is driving me crazy!" We found out that this area we lived in was once an airport and before that it had been an Indian burial ground. Who knows? It's hard to explain these strange incidences, but here is my thinking: Why do some people have certain experiences and others don't? Because we draw our reality to ourselves. If I have a belief that strange things are out there, I will have these experiences. Another person might move into that house and not have weird stuff happen. I would love to talk to people who lived there after we moved, to see if they heard or saw anything strange. I wonder if I was the only one to experience these occurrences because my journey was a spiritual one.

One night I had a dream, during that in between place of not asleep but not awake, either. I had awakened on a vast stage enveloped in an intense spotlight. Everything around me was dark, and I was in a fetal position. I did not know where I was or even who I was.

A voice in the darkness said, "Who are you?"

"I don't know," I answered.

"Can you sing?"

"I don't know, I don't even know what singing is."

"Can you dance?"

"I don't know."

"Can you act?"

"I don't know. I don't even know what acting is."

"Then get off my stage until you learn."

So, I got off the stage to begin my journey. I learned every other person's dance and every other person's song, but no one could teach me how to act. I returned to the stage and said I had learned how to dance and sing, but I still hadn't learned how to act.

The voice in the dark said, "Go back out and learn how to dance your own dance, sing your own song and act."

Returning to the stage, I spoke into the darkness and said, "I have learned how to sing my own song and dance my own dance, but I need help. I don't know how to act."

Hearing nothing from the darkness, I stood in silence waiting for an answer that never came. I left the stage feeling rejected, alone, and abandoned, when a voice inside of me said, "Now you know your act."

I had many more questions for the voice in the dark. I wanted to go back to the stage for answers but was afraid to ask. And, then I thought, why am I afraid? Is fear just another act?

I jumped back on the stage and speaking into the darkness I asked, "Are you God? If this is your stage, am I playing a role that you chose for me? If God is within me, is it God who needs to be fixed? Am I just a repair man looking for special parts? I WANT TO KNOW WHY YOU MADE ME SHORT AND OVERWEIGHT WITH A FLAT ASS! Is this a punishment? Did I do something wrong in a past life or am I unique and special? I am so confused.

The voice in the dark was silent.

I left the stage guessing that I would spend the rest of my life experiencing and looking for answers, and then realized that this was my act after all. I went back to the stage to share with the voice that I had learned my lesson. The blessing is not only in the knowing, but in the experience. I cannot receive the blessing of wisdom until I embrace the experience of oneness. No understanding, no wisdom, neither exists until knowing and experience come together. We all are one, sharing our uncommon experiences and knowledge, trying to tap into the world's collective consciousness in order to discover wisdom.

I have talked about angels and teachers being all around us in our lives. Awakening comes when we start to recognize them and their value. I believe that when a "student" is ready, a "teacher" will come and the lessons will begin.

An example: a woman friend of mine, Linda, is an executive secretary with an immediate assistant and a large support staff to supervise. Her assistant is a constant irritant, causing much drama in their relationship. Linda finds fault in this woman's leadership strategies and lets her know it. The assistant is reluctant to change and becomes defensive when corrected.

When I went in to Guidance and asked for help. I was told that when Linda was a child, she lacked acknowledgment from her parents. And, by the way, this is a situation many of us have. Take a look at yourself and see if your own behavior and self-worth reflects this. Most of us need to hear that we are valued from our loved ones or those we admire. We don't often arrive in our current lifetimes with a positive sense of ourselves, so the opinions of other people matter.

The woman Linda was so irritated with also needed acknowledgment. Guidance let me know that the assistant was doing a great job with the support staff, and they loved working with her. The assistant and the support staff were vibrating at the same level. They understand each other, and they could hear her. Linda was not at their level. In order to resolve the mismatched vibrations, Linda needed to find the wisdom to give her assistant the acknowledgment she craved. By giving it to the assistant, she also gave it to herself. We are all one. Linda knows she needs acknowledgment as she is experiencing what that looks like through her assistant—and she had to reach the understanding, the wisdom that she must give in order to get.

The assistant, it turned out, was a marvelous teacher/angel for Linda.

A few years ago, I had an awful bout of stomach trouble. I was unable to enjoy eating and suffered greatly when I did. Ray and I were out for dinner one evening when I experienced an "Ah ha!" moment. I knew that I was one with all, but I was having trouble wanting to eat the dinner I had carefully selected, knowing that nothing would really set well, and I would feel rotten by the time we got home no matter what I ate. Then I looked around at the diners enjoying their food without being sick. I thought, *My God, do they know how blessed they are to be able to eat and not get sick?*

A voice came to me and said, "You are blessed because *you* know."

• • •

As a person born poor and dark-skinned, I was programmed from the time I was a new entity to feel second-rate. To feel the sting and burn of *having less than*, while at the same time, as the object of racism, *being* less than. And then to work my way out of my insecurities. That was my mission. I had to learn how to love when I had never felt loved. I had to figure out how to dance without having learned to walk.

Let's think about compassion and what it really is. Simply, it is caring and understanding that each human comes with a specific life experience, which means their thoughts and actions have equal validity and purpose. We all matter.

As well, we all have access to what I like to call Source. Source is what powers us, no matter what name we give to it. As many definitions of Source exist as there are belief systems. Catholics call on Jesus, Muslims call on Mohammed, Buddhists rely on the teachings of Buddha. I understand Source as that ancient wisdom we call instinct. It is the collective consciousness of our ancestors, which is accessible to all through meditation. Connecting to Source allows us to stand apart from the Ego, not to disconnect from Ego but to identify with the part of Self that is not ego-based or fear-based.

For instance, let's say what I crave is for someone to love me. If I am in a relationship and am being criticized by that person, I have come to understand that what he truly wants is to be acknowledged. So, I love that person by acknowledging him. If he says he doesn't like the way I comb my hair, instead of being hurt and offended, I ask how he would like me to comb it. I don't have to change a thing if I let him know he is heard—and that's all. I must stop fighting back and acknowledge. If I am feeling judged, my energy flags, if I acknowledge the other person's need and move on, I have learned to keep my own light turned on, my energy high. The concept: I love me so I can love you.

We are responsible for keeping our own energy high. If we think we need someone else to generate energy, our lights will eventually go out. It isn't about giving in. It is about being in control of ourselves and creating our own power. I believe that marriage is divine, our mates are put in our lives to show the lessons we are working on. When we are married, we become one entity, and we share energy. At times we may judge the other, dimming their light. Since our energy matches, their angry response makes us feel empty and as a result, our light dims. Energy spirals downward when we are angry. Since our being is made of energy, in order to feel good, feel peaceful, we need to keep that energy up. When someone else lowers our energy, over time we become depleted, so we walk away to find another energy source. We tend to make the other person wrong so we can be right. Would you rather be right or peaceful? Pay attention to what lessons you are being shown (look at what you are judging). We spend much of life yearning to be loved and acknowledged when what we are truly learning is *to love* and to find inner peace.

Connecting to Source provides clarity, joy, strength, humor, compassion—building blocks for shaping a harmonious love affair with yourself. The connection is not outside of you but within you and is essential to happiness and health and loving yourself unconditionally.

After all, I can be a bitch and still be the loving and lovable person I am. Who says bitchy is bad and being a nice girl is the correct way to be? It is just an opinion. Source, which knows and sees all, sees us as perfection and loves us infinitely and completely.

• • •

I think of Source as being just like Pacific Gas & Electric (PG&E). I have PG&E connected to my house, and if I want a light to turn on, I flip a switch to connect to the source of power. In the case of Source, I *am* the power that turns on my Source light.

And I do it with thought.

A woman I did a psychic reading for was upset with her husband. She was coming to see me because she was tired of feeling like she was getting no emotional support from him. The husband was void of feeling because he never had had the emotional support he needed as a child. I didn't get the sense of depression in him, rather that he had checked out of conscious living. During this same period, his father was in the process of dying. The husband didn't know how to feel and was looking for support, but he didn't know that about himself, either. His wife was looking for emotional support, but she knew this. What she didn't know is that she was demanding emotional support from a man who did not have it to give to begin with.

A big mess. Now that his father was dying, the husband had effectively left the building. Feeling emotions at this juncture was too painful, so he put them to sleep. Some people do it by staring at porn. This guy had turned off an internal switch, his connection to Source. Both man and wife were dimming each other's lights. Together they had become stagnant. Who between them would awaken to shake things up? She might have to leave him, not permanently, perhaps, but long enough for him to begin healing and to understand that he misses her, that he does still love her. He needed to feel the aloneness that she felt inside the marriage. Isn't it interesting how powerful we are! We can literally check out if things are too painful, and from the outside, no one in the greater world is the wiser. Except those closest to us.

I have been asked, if I were given a second chance at this life, what would I do differently? Easy answer—I would listen with an open mind. In my early years, I listened with my mind snapped closed. I already had my ideas and opinions firmed up and stamped with my own approval. But I wonder what I missed. Most of the time I might have pretended to listen, but my closed mind missed the opportunity to take in another human's fresh perspective.

For example, if I were having a conversation with a person who supported a different political party than I do, and she was giving a sales pitch for her beliefs, I wouldn't hear her at all. My mind wandered as I absently faked interest. I'd already figured out my beliefs, so I was not interested in hers. Another example is a parent talking to their child. The parent is trying to let the child know that smoking is a terrible idea for many reasons, and the child, who is in the clutches of his peers, is nodding at words, wishing for his parent to stop talking.

The creation of a whole human being takes a lifetime, mainly because we so often listen with a closed mind.

• • •

In this life, we must balance ourselves between the two—playing the role but staying aware of Source. If we can do this, we can live in balance, in compassion, and share our pure love and true identity with the world. It is balance that allows us to consciously manifest our desires in life. You might be a kick-ass businesswoman, but your soul is love and compassion. Both sides are equally valuable. We are human and spirit at the same time and to ignore either side of the equation is to bring about imbalance and discord. To be compassionate, you must find the harmonious center of yourself in that space between the human being and the spiritual or Source energy. This is what being centered means, and when you are centered, you are balanced. In that balance you find compassion.

I had a conversation with friends one day. I was talking about a homeless-looking man on the street who tried to talk to me. I reached a twenty-dollar bill toward him instead, which he waived away, saying he only wanted to talk. Not willing to give my time, I walked away.

Later, feeling guilty, I relayed the story to a friend who said, "Why don't you do like we do and just take him in to eat?"

I said "I can't make those kinds of judgments."

The friend said, "Connie, I am not judging the person, but I would rather take him to eat than give him twenty dollars to buy beer."

This irritated me. Assuming a homeless man might use money to buy beer was making a judgment. Assuming he was hungry was judgment, too. But there *I* was, judging a person who thought he knew the right way to help. In the meantime, I felt judged, which irritated me further. If we need to learn to be compassionate, we will be given every chance. I felt compassion for a potentially hungry man, but not for the person who thinks differently than I. In the end, the conversation left me feeling worse than I did going in.

Compassion and gratitude exist in levels within each of us. If I can be a beacon for gratitude, I don't have to think about it. I am by nature a grateful person—that is just me. Also, two lives can come together with the same wisdom and the same message even among people of distinctively different backgrounds. To be in the flow, in the moment of who we are, we must exist in love and compassion *and* gratitude. As you grow, you come to recognize this level of flow because it because it feels so darned good.

My belief is that judgment creates resistance, which blocks energy and our pathway to Source, which then creates karma. Karma is a lesson that repeats when we don't learn it the first time. We are not here to judge another's journey, but to let our judgments show us what needs to be cleansed in ourselves. Allowing others to *just be* helps to create peace, but the formula is more complicated than that. The whole of it is this: gratitude creates joy, and joy raises vibration. Vibration creates prosperity, and prosperity creates fullness. Fullness, then, creates peace.

WHEN THE STUDENT IS READY, THE TEACHER ARRIVES

I never understood any part of being spiritual until we moved to Benicia, and I met Betty Bethards. Meeting Betty was the best thing to happen to me, outside of Ray and my daughter Deborah, and the timing was just right.

At first, I thought she was a little off the wall, but here is what started happening. I was at a certain level of spiritual development, and wasn't totally comfortable with what I was learning. Then, my psychic channel started opening, and I began receiving information that was foreign and hard to understand. I attended Betty's lectures every month. At these lectures, she *just happened* to back up information I had received from channeling Source.

The first time I realized this, I was talking to a client while channeling and told the person, "When you grow spiritually, your eyes change." Later, I went to Betty's lecture on the first Monday of the month, and she looked right at me. I felt time stand still as she said, "You know, when you grow spiritually, your eyes change," and then she went on with her lecture.

This started happening on a regular basis, as if I were being reassured. No one else heard what I heard—I don't think. Strange experiences like that were coming to me. At some point, I began to look forward to the messages and eventually to expect them.

Meeting Betty Bethards was meant to be. There I was, new in town, didn't know where to go, and I was bored. I took a drive to The Willows, an outdoor shopping center in Concord, about a fifteen-minute drive, to pass the time by walking around. A handful of women stood chatting in a tiny dress shop when I walked in, with one woman behind a desk. They were talking about Betty Bethards. Two of them were asking the woman behind the desk if she planned to attend Betty's lecture.

I wasn't really listening because I didn't know who this Betty person was. But—and I will never forget this—I was looking at blouses and one of the gals spoke up and said, "Oh Betty Bethards, I just had a psychic reading from her."

Well, of course my ears perked up. I then remembered hearing her name at the beauty shop I worked in. What are the odds that I would wind up in a tiny dress store that I had never visited before, where a row of angels was set up just for me?

Events like this are called vibrational magic. In one of her lectures, Betty talked about being in the dream state in which we are outside the body and are being taught from the other side. I thought, "Give me a break, I'm not buying that at all." But then one morning, I was lying in bed asleep thinking that I needed to shut the alarm off. About that time the alarm went off and I lay there and watched my arm—which looked like a puff of smoke shaped like my arm—reach out and hit the alarm. It dawned on me that Betty was right. I recognize the fact that I have had multiple versions of these vibrational magic experiences so that I would come to believe what I was learning. Betty had said we are being taught constantly whether we are awake or asleep. I think at times when you wake up and are still tired, it is because you've been busy all night training on the other side.

Because of this, when I first went to her for a reading, I no longer felt that Betty was "out there." She came across as comfortable and her words easy to accept. She was the first to say that she was learning also. She never made herself out to be more important than anyone else. She lived her teachings, but with all of her wisdom she admitted she still had lessons to learn. She was my angel-teacher-guide that took me to the level I am at now. Did she know it? No. Do any of us realize we are teachers for another person? Sometimes, but mostly we aren't aware at all.

Once, I said to Betty, "Something strange has happened. People I'm doing readings for have become very spiritual." It was true. More and more I was hearing from people who described themselves as being on a spiritual path. She explained that this was happening because *I* had shifted; I had raised my level of consciousness, so I was drawing in people who needed help at that level. I have heard it said, "If you want your relationship to change, change your relationship with yourself." When you learn that giving and receiving are one, you begin to see the illusion in life. I heard it said that "illusion is perspective." We have the power to change what is in front of us. Once you shift your consciousness, your life shifts. If you want love, be loving. If you want to be heard, listen, and so forth. We are born perfect, then we become part of this world, and we learn from the people and culture we are immersed in, and we create our way of thinking. Next, we are ripe to judge those who don't think like we do. As we create our lessons, we attract the person or thing or situation that will teach us what we need to learn. We see in those people or experiences what we need to see, an illusion.

For instance, you meet the person and decide to marry. The wedding day is the height of your joy, then a certain amount of reality sets in. You have to share, there are habits you didn't see before, the in-laws are a trial. Reality dims the light, and we begin to judge. Once we see the lesson, however, the judgment falls away. Ray loved to gamble, and it was my illusion that if he loved me, he wouldn't gamble. But that was an illusion from my own reality where gambling was bad. What I needed to see was him as a loving human being and not judge him for his habits. This is called vibrational matching: we become magnets for people whose vibration matches ours. A good example of this is my favorite metaphysical store in downtown Benicia called Angel Heart 4 You. Carol Mayer re-opened it in 2009, and she attracts psychics from the area. Maybe it is the case that we are the only ones who are aware that the store even exists. People who are interested in such things see it because their eyes are open to it, but I often wonder if it is even visible or if it registers at all with those who are not at Carol's level of vibration.

I believe vibrational matching explains why some relationships are short-lived. Nothing holds them together. People are only in our lives long enough to lead us to whatever our lesson is. In my younger days, when I was emotionally insecure, I drew people to me who were the same. I know almost none of those people now. As I grew more spiritual and reached higher levels of consciousness, I drew in people like Betty Bethards.

Also, through meditation, we can come to understand when it is time to let go of people in our lives. An example: the fellow I had gone to work for at the hair salon in Benicia and I didn't get along. When I connected with Guidance during meditation, I saw my boss under a spotlight. I asked him why we didn't get along and he said, "Because this light isn't big enough for two prima donnas."

I knew immediately what my lesson was, I was a prima donna, and I had to learn to acknowledge others. If we want to be acknowledged, we must acknowledge. What is interesting is that this guy was a sweet man, and we shared several similarities. For one, we both had the tendency not to let go. He did hair differently than I did, and of course, I wanted to "fix" him—I was a beautician!

Three areas of consciousness exist: intuitive, psychic, and spiritual.

<u>Intuitive</u> is what we feel through the emotional body. It can be a feeling or a thought and can come through the energy of another.

Intuition is guidance from the ancients in action. It moves beyond the five senses.

<u>Psychic</u> is not related to emotion but can be heard through feelings, thought, or through imagination. It can present during dream state and as those *AHA!* insights we get. It can also be defined as a paranormal experience, psychic bridge, intuition, or spiritual connection. People who come to me for readings are at a spiritual level that bridges to mine, which is what propels them to seek me out. Before a person arrives at the highest spiritual level, they use intuition to interpret life and themselves. They are into feelings and recognize intuition as the body's wisdom, that the physical and intuitive body work together.

<u>Spiritual</u> refers to The Higher Self. You will hear your spiritual self through thought and inner vision—the higher creative mind. It is pure, clear thought, and is without judgment. This moves beyond the sixth sense to a higher level of wisdom. Trust that wisdom as your truth; yours and no one else's. The more focus, the more power you give to the higher part of self, the easier it is to hear truth and wisdom. When we reach a centered place, these three levels function as one.

Reaching the higher levels of consciousness, we begin to realize something else going on here. That was the level I had reached when I met Betty Bethards. I feel she was guided into my life, and she is the one who helped me shift my consciousness. Next, without realizing it, she led me, to a new, higher level of knowing.

When we are asleep, we are also in training. Dreams and their symbols are loaded with lessons. We are in waking and sleeping school at all times and are being taught all the time at a multiple of levels. The psyche is where we connect with our higher consciousness, where this highest of levels of human consciousness can bring in symbols for us to interpret and learn from. On this "bridge" we are given symbols to interpret. Symbols in sleeping dreams can be hard to remember. Because we have this psychic bridge, we also receive symbols while we are awake, and every now and then we will pick up on them, noticing things that are a little outside of what we think of as normal. "Ah that bird shit on that window over there, what's that all about?" If I were in a sleeping dream, I would know it was a symbol. In my waking dream I have to stop, notice, and consider it as a symbol. Symbols are all around us. They carry messages and information. We need to search and analyze awake time for them, as well as sleeping time.

According to Betty Bethards, any symbol book you get will work for you because Guidance/Source will put the right book on your path. Her book is based on her interpretations, but the reality is that there is no right or wrong, just what feels like a fit. I list Betty's dream symbol interpretation book at the end of this book. For me it was the right resource but also a wonderful gift of guidance.

• • •

We had suffered a loss in our family and I was feeling the sadness one morning, when I saw two birds lying in the yard. One little bird looked dead it was so still. The second lay with its head on the first one's shoulder. It touched my heart. The sweetest, saddest thing I had ever seen—they must have been mates. I called Ray in to see it. We stood, both of us crying, five feet away. Every few moments the bird lifted its head to look at its partner. We watched for at least twenty minutes. The first bird never moved. Without warning, both birds stood up and flew away!

I gasped, "Oh my God, what a message I just received!"

Nothing ever dies, so fly on with your life. If it is not our time, we don't go. We were in Las Vegas years ago, in a car with my sister, who cannot drive. Why we let her, I will never know. We came up to a stop sign, and a car zoomed toward us like a bat out of hell.

My sister started to make a left turn and I screamed, "Don't go! That car is coming too fast!" I knew we might be killed if she went. Time stood still, the car coming toward us like a slow-motion movie, my sister making her turn safely, and then everything speeded up again. It wasn't our time.

Not only symbols, but people are in our lives for a reason. Our life partners are our greatest teachers, but remember—lessons can be negative as well as positive. If someone close to you is driving you nuts, take a look at what you are resisting. That person is a representation of an issue you need to face **OR** you wouldn't be experiencing what you are experiencing. You will be helping them to learn, if that person is in a time of empowerment, because you are their teacher, as well. Resistance is what keeps us out of flow, out of feeling peaceful. Judgment is the resistance that blocks your energy source and creates karma. We are not here to judge another's journey, only to view from within judgment in order to see what needs to be cleansed in ourselves. Feeling resistance is uncomfortable, not peaceful. It shows itself as rejection, guilt, possessiveness, jealousy, and fear. If we all look back to what we first resisted in life, we will see what our life's lessons are.

It takes a life time to see these things. It is like reading a book. You think, *I get it, I really understand that book.* Then you go down the line, get older, have more experiences, and you see that now you *really* do understand what that book meant. The depth of your understanding has increased. Channeling Source, reading symbols, and meditation—these are some of my tools. Learning to use them and to tap into each level of spirituality has taken years of work.

We all are channels and all are connected to a higher energy, god-mind, or higher consciousness. You are a channel. Once you open to that higher energy, you become aware that you also have access to the same source. Channeling is information that comes as a flow of words. I refer to myself as a psychic transformation coach and multi-level channel. Through channeling, I receive information for spiritual growth and for assisting others in becoming aware of what is blocking their way. Once I have identified a client's fear, life changes, and life lessons, I can help clear those blocks and guide the person to understand any questions they have about their life's path. My client will ultimately make his or her own life-changing decisions, and that makes all the difference.

Opening up to Source can be described as having access to different radio stations. Tuning into a station and getting static can be interpreted as being focused outside of the self. We get a clear sense of who we are when we become still. In other words, we must find quiet if we are to open to this universal power source—higher energy, god-mind, Source, life force, or higher consciousness—it has many names, but no matter what you call it, it allows us to receive information or insight. Once you open those pathways, the energy from Source reflects inward. You become aware of your uniqueness, your store of knowledge, and a sense of "knowingness" within. At this point, you have access to your inner voice. You cannot listen to this inner voice if you are listening to outer voices or are focused outside of self.

Thoughts, actions, and reactions that are outside of self will deplete vital energy, as does excessive worry, anger, and fear. These create blocks. Emotional attachments scatter energy, causing static, which blocks access to higher energy. Becoming centered and drawing awareness inward brings you to the point of communicating with the self. I feel that the best way to achieve this is through daily meditation. Centeredness is where Source is. Through daily meditation, you quiet the mind, recapture scattered energy to bring it inward. In that place of quiet centeredness, you contact Source and can channel guidance.

Years ago, when I first started understanding spirituality, I went to classes where people were seeing spirit guides who were

Indians, some with ponies, some beating drums, wearing war paint, etc. I wondered why I wasn't seeing spirit guides who were Indians. The reason is that the Indian image was not a part of me or my experience or interest. The people who saw Indians wanted to. Native American culture and spirituality had people's attention at the time. Native symbolism was everywhere. That shifted, and Buddha became popular, and everybody began seeing Buddha.

Really, it doesn't matter what a guide looks like or what comes through, it matters that we hear our inner voice. Everything is imagination based on experience, karmic or current. Everything is our own illusion, how we see and interpret what we are seeing. Interpretations coming from Source are always right because I am tapped into this collective consciousness. If I am not centered and connected, then I could interpret it incorrectly, but if I am in my higher self, there is *no way* I can be wrong. I ask for the Divine Light of love and compassion to surround me, and when it does, I can feel it, and I know I am channeling. When I am centered in the Divine Light I could say, "Go to hell, bitch!" And you would hear "you are lovely." It doesn't matter what I say, you would hear what you need to hear. This is hard to teach because, like it or not, we are all stuck in our egos, wanting to be right.

As a channel, you can't get caught up in analyzing what is coming through. You have to trust that Divine energy is doing the talking. We are always being "watched" by a Source that feels nothing but love and adoration for us. Source never judges and is always listening *and hearing* us, seeing us as perfect just the way we are. When there is a need for a lesson, Source works with us to balance our desires with our limitations. Angels assist us at all times, and they have no expectations of us whatsoever, for they can see us clearly and from all sides. If we believe we can have what we desire, angels are always working to allow the manifestation. They will offer us miracles if we will allow them. We are powerful—we just don't know it. We have the power of choice and that makes all the difference. In our imaginations, we have the power and the freedom to see things and experience them in whatever way we choose, but Source holds the truth, and in the long run, even if we hold ourselves apart from that truth for a lifetime, we will return to it eventually. Source never disconnects from us. When we die, we unhook from our physical bodies, which we have chosen for this life, but not from our souls.

Human reality is such that we want to see, feel, and touch in order to believe. When someone comes in to my consciousness, I am not seeing a person standing there. The sensation is one of *knowing*. If a client asks me to describe the person, I could say he is tall, barefoot, and has a smile on his face. We are pure energy, and when I am meditating or channeling, I feel that energy. If you are my client and you want to see the person, you can in your imagination. I can describe enough that the person will walk into your imagination. I cannot see the guide or the person spoken of, I simply know they are there. You have to see it yourself because only you can attach to your experience and provide details, based on what you already know.

I say, "See your guide step forward." I believe our lives are our creation, and I will create my life through my imagination. If you look back over your life, it has been what you wanted it to be. It was your driving force that brought it all into being, even negative life choices. Think about what you set up for yourself to learn.

Good story. A man came to see me because he had a dream, and he was really upset. He was going to invest a hundred thousand dollars. This was a long time ago and then this was an extreme amount of money. He had a dream and his father, who had passed over, said in the dream "Don't buy that stock!"

The man was confused, he felt like it was good stock, but his dad had told him not to buy. I asked him what kind of a relationship he had with his dad. He said they fought all the time. They had a volatile relationship. I asked if he listened to his dad, and he said no, he didn't. Then, don't listen to him now, I told him. He bought the stock. The dad was working with him from the other side. In this man's dream, his dad was telling not to buy the stock because he knew he wouldn't listen. He was trying to talk to him in a language he could hear. The guy wound up making a lot of money. The dad was an angel for his son.

• • •

We can see beginnings, and we can see endings. For so many years I was just a face in the crowd to Betty Bethards. A friend stopped by one night and invited me to attend a lecture of Betty's. I hadn't been in a year or so. When we arrived, I was shocked to see the crowd was so small when normally they were huge. We got there early, and my friend got in line to get a reading from Betty. I went to buy four of her dream analysis books. I stood in a corner by myself, flipping through the dream books, when she walked over to me.

"Would you like for me to sign those for you?" she said.

In all the years I had gone to see her, I'd never gotten a book signed. She signed all four copies for me. On stage that night I saw no aura around her at all. She was very powerful, and I could always see an aura around her. She died a few weeks after that. I will never forget her walking over to me to sign those books. It was a closure, an ending. As you can imagine, I treasure those books, and always will.

I had learned much from Betty. She had taught me one-to-one but didn't know it. I miss her very much. I resonated with her. She wasn't pretentious, had no ego, just a rusty old can. In her early days, she smoked cigarettes and drank Pepsi constantly. She would walk outside to do readings and people followed her outside so she could smoke. She was full of wisdom, human as well as spirit. The balance was visible.

With so many other lecturers I could not see a balance, only ego. The message was, "I am spiritual, so let's go walk on hot coals. Let's get naked." None of that made sense to me, but Betty did. What a blessing to have known her as a teacher and to have been her student.

As your teachers come, and your journey moves along, know that not everyone in your life will support it. This story is about a couple Ray and I traveled with. We had become friends years ago, having met in one of my classes. She was working for a large company, and they would take Ray and I on trips the company partially paid for. Vacations are nice.

Over the years she would quote me, "Connie said this, Connie said that." I started to notice her coming over alone, him staying home. I asked where he was, and she'd say he was a little grumpy, so he stayed home. The last time we traveled with them, she called and said, "Connie, I really have to talk to you, something just happened." She came to our room and told me she had just been fired. She received a call saying that her job had been eliminated. As she was talking, I saw her working at a bigger company, so I said for her not to worry about it, that she would have a job in January, would know about it in December, and this job would be far greater than the one she had now. She had no need to worry.

She had been sad, and her husband had been consoling her. She returned to her room, happy, and told him, "Connie told me not to worry. A better job is coming—dahda dahda dah."

He said, "Do you really still believe in that shit?" Remember, he used to come to my classes and read Tarot cards.

She said, "What do you mean?"

He barked, "If you need to talk to somebody, you talk to me."

This was a huge lesson for me. She made me too important, and he felt intimidated. She did get that fabulous job in December and started working in January at Genentech. Had she not been fired, she wouldn't have gotten the better job. Another lesson. Change can be good.

• • •

I went to work one day and my co-worker Pat said, "Connie, I talked to a client and she mentioned a course you might be interested in. I can't remember the name. I'll have to think about this."

Over the weekend, I had a dream, and when I awoke on Monday morning, I heard a voice say, "Miracle."

I told Ray that morning that we were going to have a miracle. I always pay attention to that transition time when I am first waking up. Pat called later that morning, and I reminded her that she was going to try to think of the name of the course.

She said, "Let's go have lunch, and afterward I will try to find the place where that course is being taught."

We had lunch and went out to find the place. No idea where we were going. We were just out to have fun, and Pat was following her nose. She insisted over and over that I would like this course, and she was certain the building was in Pleasant Hill, not fifteen minutes from Benicia.

Eventually, she found the building, a holistic practices store, and we went inside.

Of course, you know that over the door hung a sign that read, "This is your miracle."

Pat perused a bookshelf and saw the book, *A Course in Miracles*. I asked the woman who worked there about the book, and she said they hosted that class every Monday afternoon.

As I said, this was Monday. We went in knowing nothing, had never even seen the book before. People started arriving and finding their seats. The woman started the session and asked what lesson we should start with. Pat asked if they could start on lesson one because we had never been before. The guy sitting next to me was getting so pissed, he was starting to huff and puff, and I am thinking, "Why would he be so angry?"

Finally, he jumped up and said, "Let's sing!"

Pat and I looked at each other, not knowing what the hell was going on.

He looked at us and yelled, "Get up and sing!"

We sang! Sweetly, we sang "Halleluiah, Halleluiah" as he was screaming it. He did not want us to come into this group or to have the group start from the beginning. How dare we! We left there laughing like hell, what an experience.

On the way home, I told Pat that I didn't think that was my miracle. *A Course of Miracles* is complex and hard to decipher, much like the Bible. It is written so that if three people are reading it, they will have three different ideas about what each lesson means. This is what makes it great—it fits all readers. Even so, I was sure this was not the course for me.

The next day, I was at work at the beauty shop, and a client asked if I had heard of *A Course in Miracles* The next day! I said, yes, but that I had a very strange experience with it. I told her about these crazy people going on with all of this judgment.

She said, "Oh Connie, that's not what it is about. My mother teaches the course at Unity Center. Why don't you go there and see what it's about?"

I thought, "Okay, I will go see what it is all about."

I did go. I met my client's mother, and it was a completely different experience. I learned that the woman who wrote the book was an atheist psychologist. She had started hearing a voice. She was channeling and didn't know it. She was talking to one of the professors she worked with and told him she thought she was going crazy. She was getting much information, amazing information, that she didn't know what to do with. When she shared what she was hearing, he told her to write it down.

A Course in Miracles tells us, "Once you see what you need to see it is no longer there." I have found that to be true. Also, "seek not to change the world, but change your mind about the world," and "perception is a result and not a cause." Most sought after writers of spiritual growth, regardless of faith, refer to *A Course in Miracles*.

• • •

Mom died before we left Stockton for Benicia, and I was full of guilt. We had a terrible fight, and she died the next night. Ray and I started arguing, and we were having a terrible time. When he'd had enough, he left. I didn't know where the hell he was, and I didn't care.

That was on a Monday. Tuesday, my friend called and asked me to attend a "Course" class that night. I told her I wasn't in the mood, and she said that if I changed my mind, it started at 7:30. At 7:00 I changed my mind and went. Guess what the topic was that night? Anger. The class totally shifted my consciousness. I had no desire to be around people. My anger was intense, but I couldn't truly say what I was angry about. After the class, I was reborn into a peaceful human being. When Ray came home that weekend in his Hawaiian shirt and surfer shorts, saying "Guess where I've been?" I was happy to see him. He acted shocked to realize that I wasn't the same mad person he had left. I came to realize that my anger with Ray was centered on my guilt over the fight with my mother and my need to be right. Anger overlaid my guilt.

Right after that my channel zoomed open. I started crying one day, which was unusual. I have never been a crier, but I couldn't stop. As I cried, a voice channeled through telling me that I was working through guilt. I needed my mother's acknowledgment, and she needed mine. She couldn't acknowledge me because I couldn't acknowledge her. This created resistance. We were in resistance all of those years because we were sharing the same lesson. That was my biggest lesson in illusion. I need acknowledgement from my mother. She loved me and worked her ass off feeding and caring for me. How nice it would have been if I could have told her that before she died. That I understood.

Of course, things happened exactly as they should have. I went through this whole transformation; Mom passed away. Betty Bethards arrived in my life, and *A Course in Miracles* opened my eyes. These things happened at the exact moment I was ready to learn from them.

I've said this before: our families are our teachers. I look at my life now and can't believe I didn't see it earlier. My purpose has been in my face my whole life. I'm called to share love, compassion, and understanding. My parents were my first teachers, then Ray, then my daughters, Deborah, Mary, and Pam. There was a time when I felt that my mother acknowledged my sister Ruby much more than she did me. Ruby had run away, and we never saw her again, simple as that. One day I got so tired of hearing my mother talk about Ruby and I said," Mom, goddammit, you are always talking about Ruby when you've got other kids to worry about. I didn't know Ruby. I was still a toddler when she left, but I had no patience when it came to the subject of Ruby, and boy did I ever have to walk that karma later in my life.

My Deborah got married in Tunisia, so we had to get passports. In the 1930s, no migrant worker's baby was born in a hospital, and our constant moving confused our birth information even more. In order to get to Deborah's wedding, I had to have a passport, and to get a passport I had to have a birth certificate. Ray was trying to help.

When we were little, we never lived near churches, so my mom became our minister, and she would sit us down and preach to us. Always compassionate, she would never turn away anyone who was hungry. She taught us, her children, never to turn away anyone because it might be Jesus Christ.

During our search for my birth certificate or baptismal record, I remember a funny story. One day, I was seven or so, and we were living in an old house by the railroad tracks. We always lived in old houses by the railroad tracks. In those days, people we called hobos rode the rails. I don't remember where my mom had gone, but she left me to watch a pot of beans. A man knocked on the door and said he was hungry, asking if we had work that he might do in exchange for a meal. Of course, I thought, OH MY GOD IT'S JESUS CHRIST! He came in and wound up eating all the beans. He spooned them in, and I kept filling his bowl. After all, I had been taught—well, you know.

My mom came in and wanted to know what happened to our dinner, what happened to the beans.

"Well, Mom," I said. "Jesus Christ was here today and he ate all the beans."

She damned near exploded, "WHAT! You let somebody in this house?"

"Mom, it was Jesus Christ, he was hungry!"

It was the beginning of my confusion over formal religion. When you live an isolated life with no television, just a shared radio and no other outside influences—you believe what your mom says without question.

Even though Mom hadn't raised us in church, at some point I was baptized. Ray went to the town of Fairfield where I was baptized to get my baptismal records, but my name was spelled wrong. Since I was raised with my stepfather's last name, my school records were under Connie Rafael, not Connie Castro. To make things worse, my mother had spelled my first name as Concellita or something similar and for some reason filled in the wrong birthdate and the wrong place of birth. She said I was born in Sunnyvale, but Cherry Castro, my real dad, had told me I was born seventy miles away in the San Joaquin Valley.

The only thing I know from my sister is that my aunt delivered me. My mother said Dad was not there, but he says he was. In my anger that day I called her and said, "Mom, you didn't even know my goddam name, you didn't know where I was born—what is this?" Of course, to me it was the ultimate example of her not acknowledging me. I don't remember her reply, just my indignation and more resistance.

Ray and I talked to a lawyer, and after making some suggestions that didn't work, she said, "Okay, here is what you do. Find an old Bible and have your mother use different ink for each child and write everybody's birthdates in this Bible. In those days, that was how births were recorded. I thought—where in hell do I get an old Bible?

A couple of days later, I was talking to a client about the issue, and she said "I have one!" She gave me her old Bible, Mom added the names and dates, and the lawyer accepted it as proof of birth.

To look back and see who your teachers and guides are and have been; who you have learned from, is enlightening. When Ray and I were first married, I thought his two girls were jealous of me, and I would get irritated at them. It wasn't until years later that I realized I was the jealous one. I had never in my life felt myself a part of the whole. The existence of those two girls made me feel pushed me out of the family, at least what I thought a family should feel like. But it was only because I didn't know how to share. I couldn't share Ray. Now of course I know his girls, who are grown into women, were compassionate and understanding. I can look back and see this. Lessons often appear as mistakes or failures. Failing to *ever* learn the lesson is the only true mistake.

Connie's mother, Josie, as a young bride in Oklahoma

The only picture of Connie as a baby,
with her big sister Ruth in 1938

Connie's mother Josie (L) with Ruth, approx. 1946

Connie with her father Cherry Castro

A blonde Connie with 4-year-old Deborah, 1964

The Jackson sisters as teens: Mary (L), Pam (C), Deborah (R)

Deborah, 2007

Deborah 2008

Connie and Ray

The Jacksons in 2014: from the left
Mary, Connie, Ray, and Pam

Connie

EVERYTHING IS ENERGY AND VIBRATION

In a Stockton, California, hospital on March 2, 1960, I gave birth to my perfect little Pisces. Ray sat in the waiting room, since fathers weren't allowed to be a part of the delivery in those days, which meant I had a few minutes alone, overwhelmed by a flood of love and fear. How was I to care for a baby? I knew little about the situation I was in. What does it take to be a good mother? How do I protect her? As a teen, I had vowed never to have children. I saw my mother's hard life providing for eleven kids on a farmworker's wage—no way I was going to end up like her.

But then I fell in love with the tiny girl. Ray was a natural parent. He knew just what to do and was the one who changed her and dressed her for the ride home from the hospital.

Deborah turned out to be a comfortable child to raise. Wise beyond her years, even at an early age, she surprised me with her deep thoughts. She loved animals, and at three years old, during dinner one night, she asked," Mommy, do you think it is an awful thing to eat animals?"

I said I didn't know, but if she didn't want to eat meat, it was okay.

She said she just wanted to know. It didn't surprise me, however, when as an adult, she became a vegetarian.

Deborah met her future husband at San Francisco State University. They both worked in the bookstore. One day the store manager got after Deborah and Hani took him on. They hadn't met before that moment, but he jumped to her defense, and soon they began dating. She was studying for her teaching credential and then a counseling degree. They became a couple, graduated from college, and lived together several years, mostly in Southern California, before marrying. Hani was from Palestine. Problems in the Middle East between Palestinians and Israelis were boiling over. The wedding took place in Sidi Bou Said, Tunisia. As Americans, Hani was nervous about our family traveling there, telling us to be careful about what we said and did. Since Ray and I did not speak the language and didn't know the customs, we had to rely on Deborah and Hani for pretty much everything. It was nerve-wracking day in and day out to be walking on eggshells. Even the usually happy bride was careful and quiet.

When we got to the church, we saw that Hani's mother and sisters had planned and prepared the whole wedding. Ray and I were shocked to learn that Hani's mother was Christian, and the minister American. Hani's family took over, dressing my daughter, doing her hair, and getting her prepared. Clearly no one intended for me to be involved. Certainly not the ideal wedding I had wanted for my Deborah. I felt left out and sad to be on the sidelines. Probably no one suspected how I felt. Neither Ray, Deborah, nor I said a word, as worried about ruffling feathers as we were.

Deborah was beautiful, her dress simple, elegant, street-length, and made of lace. The soft off-white contrasted nicely with her glossy brown hair.

From our hotel window, we saw incredibly beautiful buildings painted blue and white. One morning, we stood outside on the street, taking it all in, when a team of horses with riders came our way. Stunning, huge, black stallions, decorated and shining, carried horsemen dressed like they belonged *Arabian Nights*. My god, those men were handsome. I will never forget it.

Knowing we had a big reception planned when we got home softened some of the hurt from being left out of Deborah's wedding. Her bubbly, happy personality was on full display that day. Those hazel brown eyes finally snapping with joy and humor as she made her rounds, greeting and welcoming our family and friends.

Ray and I never went back to the Middle East, but Deborah and Hani visited over the years, and their daughter has travelled there several times. Their marriage lasted eighteen years, and the best result is their daughter Josie, named for my mother. Deborah and Ray discussed politics, current events, mutual interest. Equals in terms of intelligence, pretty much everything interested them. Life interested them. The two would sit at the kitchen table together, talking and laughing for hours. I might as well have been in another room. One evening, I could not get a word in, so I said, "Good night, I'm off to bed." And you know, they never noticed! I could have been choking on a bone for Christ's sake. Ray was proud of Deborah, and she lived up to his pride. She loved her daddy. He got such a kick out of his sweet, kind girl who could stand up for herself. With a smile, he would regularly say that it took a lot to make her angry, but if someone got on her bad side, she would not hesitate to straighten them out.

• • •

A young lady, age about thirty, came to see me one day, very interested in my classes. She asked what they were about. I told her the guts of it was spiritual, which made her nervous.

I asked what her belief system was, and she replied, "I'm Catholic."

When I asked what the Catholic belief is, she said "I believe in heaven and hell."

I shot back, "Who goes to heaven or hell?"

She answered with a question, "Spirit?" She was nervous about my class because of the word spirit. I thought it was interesting that the word made her nervous, and that when she thought about heaven or hell, she had never thought about who goes there.

She came to the next class.

Historically, religious belief systems sprout from the fear at the center of them. Always, humans have been exiled or executed for having insights beyond the understanding of the ruling class. When I first realized I had a psychic gift, almost sixty years ago, I could have been arrested for practicing and sharing spiritual information. We had to be very careful, so I'm familiar with that brand of fear.

Fear and doubt are individualized, designed, and set up by each of us. We basically decide before birth what we will fear and what we will doubt. What is truth? It feels like peace. My belief is that love is the only reality in life. The vibration of love is absolute truth, and it is the opposite of fear. All else is illusion based on our accrued knowledge and experiences.

In other words, *what the hell is this all about*?

Each person's truth is real. Each religion, at its core, contains love and compassion *as a goal* for its practitioners, even though these things are taught using fear. Truth is gentle, not angry. Fear is the root of anger. You may have noticed that people across the ages have protected their religious truths and beliefs with a good dose of anger toward those of us who do not believe the same things. The work-around is for each of us to create a "Way" or belief system of our own. A concrete physical symbol helps to give substance to our truth; we have symbols that depict Jesus but not for God. Jesus represents love and compassion. Buddhists look to the teachings of Guatama Buddha, also a symbol of love and compassion, and there are more. The GREAT ONE has no face, but the messenger always does.

Each of us creates in our minds an individualized belief system based on what we have stored in our memories from our background and experiences, and we look for symbols that communicate what we believe. I'm not interested in an individual's belief system. We aren't necessarily aware of what our filters are, so we lose objectivity and are left with nothing but a big question. If a person comes to me and wants a message from the other side, a past life, I can do a reading and provide it. The information is available, but I have no control over how that person will *receive* what comes through me. The Universe makes it easy to learn. Lessons are presented using the language of our beliefs. If my belief system changes, so will my view, but the Divine or Source still finds a way through. Hopefully now you understand when I say, what you believe doesn't matter to me.

In one of my Tuesday classes, an attendee once asked if I believe in past lives. I believe, and I don't believe, so that was my response. Another person in the group said, "Connie! I just came to you for a reading, and you talked about my past life!!" She was right, and I told her it was because she believes in past lives, that's her belief system. I have to read through each person's belief system, but the message is not affected. If you believe you lived past lives, truth can come through as a past life. A person who needs to believe in UFOs is going to see UFOs. Learning our lessons during our lifetimes is most important. The lens (belief system) through which we see is not. People believe that an old soul is one who has been reincarnated many times and has gained a certain amount of innate wisdom from those experiences. Sometimes I wonder if our energy connects farther back than the womb. My mother and I needed the same lesson. She needed me to acknowledge her as much as I needed it from her. Is it an energy string? If she didn't learn a lesson, did she pass the need for the lesson to the next generation? Or to her own next lifetime? If each soul is a link in a lineage of energy, generation to generation, that might explain karma and reincarnation. I am like my father, a showman who loved the center of attention, a storyteller—is he a part of my past life? If we are all one, connected by the collective consciousness or Source, then does each person in the progression refine the lesson? Would the lesson become more and more specific with each generation? Since we are pure energy, were my parents my generator? Did my energy arise from them, and were my thoughts born of them? Are all of us together one entity split in various splinters, so that the greater entity learns more in a shorter period of time?

Big questions. Hell, when I think about it, we have too much to learn in one lifetime. Reincarnation would be a big help.

Out of the blue one night, a woman called to ask if I would see her daughter, Melanie, who was anorexic and extremely depressed. She had seen doctors and submitted to their tests but still had no answers, no relief. This mom did not know how to help and was terrified they were running out of time. When the appointment arrived, in walked a beautiful, tiny, frail fourteen-year-old-girl. She had soft brown curls and her big, luminescent green eyes made her look like an angel. A sad little angel

We introduced ourselves, and Melanie took a seat. Hands in her lap, she sat with her head down. I felt overwhelmed by her sadness. I centered, connected with Source, and the information came through quickly. She had lived a previous life during WWII as a young Jewish girl in France. Forced to hide from the Nazis, she and her mother had no food. That incarnation of Melanie watched her mother die of starvation after the rest of her family had already perished.

Melanie wanted to know about this past life because she didn't understand why she wasn't able to deal with her current one. She seemed to draw comfort in the fact that her depression was rooted in something valid, even though it was a past life. Her current home and family were wonderful and it, didn't fit that she was miserable.

I worked with Melanie through her teens. She was a tortured soul. In many of our sessions, she spent the time writing, letting her words flow. She looked forward to it. Our energy matching filled her with enough peace to be creative. We met twice weekly, and I never charged for these sessions, I would have done whatever I could to help this girl who remained childlike even into her late teens. I never knew her to come across as an adult. She also never appeared totally present. Her mind was elsewhere. She was brilliant, but wasn't meant to be with us long. Her dream was to become a chef and even before we uncovered her past life, she felt the pull to study at the Le Cordon Bleu in France—the country where she had died in that past lifetime. She did attend the Culinary Institute of America in San Francisco and went to France for some training at Le Cordon Bleu. Her short life was filled with many parallels between her past life and the present. Here she was, anorexic with the dream to work with food, then feeling the pull to go to France where she had previously died of starvation.

Eventually Melanie reached the point where she appeared to be managing her depression and came home from her dream semester in France. Still tiny and frail, a few nights later while driving, she fainted at the wheel with her foot stuck on the accelerator. It wasn't clear if the faint episode was caused by anorexia. She died in the crash. How ironic that the lack of food may have killed her in both lifetimes.

• • •

Learning not to judge another person's belief system is one of the hardest lessons we human beings face. I say GIVE PEOPLE PERMISSION TO BELIEVE WHAT THEY WANT!

What causes the most hatred and the most war in the world? Why do we come in different colors and cultures? Why was I raised to eat rice and Ray was raised to eat bread? We are not here to judge others; we are here to learn about ourselves. Looking at differences is a wonderful teaching tool, the positive side of judging. By looking at contrasts, we can replace judgment with the fullness of peace.

What is real? Is reality only seen through the filter of our own beliefs? When was this system set up? Who set it up? Did I come into my life with a list of lessons I needed to learn, and was my belief system designed to fit those lessons? I say there is no answer. Ray always said he didn't know the answer, but he believed an answer exists. I only know what motivates me. Love and kindness work. Anger and frustration do not. We must remember that we have a spirit side and a human side. Spirit is who we are, but without our bodies, without physical and emotional feelings, we couldn't change or grow. We need life's stimulus—loss, pain, suffering, embrace, comfort, shame, guilt, love, joy, fear, embarrassment, etc., in order to perceive the lesson, to learn. Our body's wisdom is intuition, aligned with the ancients. When our body and mind vibrations match, we find peace. In the flow, in peace, we become one.

Each perspective is personal, and perception is shaped by our experiences. Our childhood stories might sound different if my sister told them. What every person calls truth *is* their truth. Your story is your story. People think spirituality is crazy because they want solid, quotable answers to life's big questions. The vibration of non-judgment is the one pure thing life offers, and even fear has no power except what we give it. Our sense of truth changes as we move from one life situation to another and perhaps it takes many lives within our current life to create the lessons we need. Each segment of existence feels different. For instance, I am not the person I was fifty or sixty years ago. I hardly recognize her. One constant has been my compassionate and loving nature. I hid the fact that I was uneducated and poor, always intimidated by education, for so many years afraid of getting hurt if I shared these realities. It took decades to become the *me* I am now, and even at this late age, I am *still* working on it.

Our spirit stays at a constant vibration but our body's vibration we can control. Love vibrates at a higher speed than hate. If our thoughts affect that vibrational energy of love, we can feel the peace as the energies align. We all know the wonderful high we feel when we are in love—it's a faster vibration. We can also feel it in our relationships. If I was at low-energy, Ray and I didn't get along. If my energy was high, he could do no wrong. Even now, when I am low, I put on happy music, dance, sing, and think happy thoughts until my energy raises.

Most of the clients I work with come to me because they are feeling empty and have reached a point in their lives where they are not happy. They question their purpose and their existence. They have traveled, bought fancy cars, live in fancy homes, and still aren't happy. We humans are junkies, always looking for the next high. But there comes a time in life when we must leave Disneyland.

That feeling of emptiness comes from what we are missing—the biggest, most essential component, the Higher Self. You've also heard me call it "Source." We tend to walk in separation from Source, without our energies aligned, despite the fact that spirit, our higher selves, our *Source*, is always with us. When I am being a co-creator with body and spirit and am in my flow, I can choose to jump out of my flow and be angry, disappointed, or rejected. If I call someone who never returns my call, I can choose to be angry, disappointed, and rejected that she once again didn't return my call, or I can communicate with my higher self and ask how I can stay in the flow, in peace, and why I am upset and angry. Why is it important that she respond to me? Why does she owe me a call just because I left her a message? Now, I am co-creating with Source and now I am getting answers. The human self is the problem—the higher self is the solution. Our higher selves wait for our human selves to catch up, to match in vibration so we can co-create. My whole journey has been finding myself. My spiritual energy stays constant while I run alongside trying to catch up. The result, if I do catch up, is inner peace.

• • •

I believe it is a universal truth that all is one. I believe everything is energy and energy is everything, vibrating at different speeds, creating solids, liquids, vapor. Energy also manifests in numbers and colors. According to Pythagoras, numeric codes are built into each of us at creation. Eventually those numbers present themselves to us, which allows the power of the numbers to be released into our lives. In other words, numbers have meaning. Numerology, the study of numbers, is an ancient wisdom and another way to look at our lives. Our birthdates, addresses, ages, and other numbers provide guidance if we seek their meaning.

Colors show a rate of vibration within your energy field and have different properties. For instance, the color gold, according to Betty Bethards, means "Christ light, love, something divine bestowed upon you, or great treasures within." If gold predominates in a dream, look on those translations to get a sense of what gold might mean for your life right now. You will sense which description fits. Along these lines, if you choose to wear a color that "looks good" on you, does it look good because your vibrations match or does the color affect your vibration? In a similar sense, when you wear your favorite color, do you feel good because of the vibrational match or did you pick the color *because* your vibration is up?

I have talked about shifting as we learn our lessons. This is a vibrational shift that comes with new perspective. When I met Betty Bethards and said, "The strangest thing has happened. Everybody who comes to me for a reading seems very spiritual," she said, "Of course. That's because you have shifted."

And I had.

One day at the beauty shop, I stormed into the back room in a terrible mood. I said to one of the girls I worked with, "I can't believe it. Why is it that when I'm a bitch every bitch in town shows up!" That stopped me, a lightbulb moment.

As soon as we shift, so does the world around us. If I vibrate with fear, I will draw an experience into my life to create fear. If I am jealous, I will attract the exact person who can reflect that back to me. Whatever I am, I will bring to me. All of this is about vibration. As soon as I shift my consciousness to that next level, I start bringing in people of that higher consciousness. This works in our relationships, too. Look at your partner and at what you are learning from that person. Now, think about what they are learning from you.

Also remember that in order to grow spiritually, we have to share ourselves, which is terrifying, because we don't want to be judged. The power is in sharing, while no power at all comes from being right.

I was young and "cute," and it was important for me to look good—that meant *perfect* to me. I wore full makeup to the grocery store, along with my merry widow and girdle. If you are under fifty, you probably don't know what these medieval contraptions are. Google them and be grateful. Wearing these, I couldn't breathe, but I looked great. I thought I was darling, even though my feet were probably swollen.

Now, I don't even know that girl—that girl with the need to look perfect so the world would love her. I've had to practice accepting the fact that I am perfect without the trappings—I take myself as I am, without judgment. It takes practice. I started by going to the store without makeup. Whatever I am, I am. If I accept myself without judgment, those around me will, too.

I have seen people change before my eyes. As I have become more loving, they have become more loving. Our children are our extensions: we share energy. As we change and grow, we open up change for them. A woman came in for a reading one day. She was "sick and tired" of her son saying that she was "so possessive and controlling that he no longer wanted to live at home." Then she started talking about her friend who was terribly possessive and controlling—to the point of wanting to end the friendship. In a flash, she saw the parallel.

• • •

I have a prayer I keep handy: *I commit myself to myself. I will practice being in spirit daily. If I want love, I will be loving. If I want to be heard, I will listen. If I want to be understood, I will be understanding. If I want peace, I will be peaceful. If my life is not in harmony, I will understand that I am not hearing my spirit. So be it.*

My strength is in my ability to identify the source of the problem right away. Often, what I hear is that people learn more in one reading with me than they learned working with a psychologist in ten years. Working from the inside out, I get to the lessons quickly.

To give a reading, I quiet my mind, then relax and visualize myself surrounded by light. I protect myself by saying; *I ask for the Divine light of love and compassion to fill and surround me, let the wisdom flow through me and Guidance to guide me. I am blessed, I am blessed, I am blessed.* As soon as I ask, I am connected with Source. I can feel it, a totally peaceful feeling, and I am completely focused. As with meditation, we go from our head to our heart. Once I have equalized the vibration between us, I feel release. As soon as I have mastered that, the person is ready to hear me. I feel safe, but fear or judgment can take me out of that center immediately. I am protected from client energy, so I can channel all day without becoming tired. I first acknowledge the client's strengths and do not address their problems. I must raise their vibration by getting them to acknowledge love and compassion. Each person's truth—no matter what they might say otherwise—is love and compassion; they just need reminding. Let's say the client is furious, really pissed, but it has nothing to do with who they are. At their essence, they are loving and compassionate. The rest are attachments. A person's gifts and their wisdom are not who they are, not at their core. In a reading, if I have tapped into their vibration of love and compassion, they will hear me. Then, I can guide them away from feelings of resistance and fear and toward clarity and spiritual peace. It has taken years of practice for me to be able to reach this meditative state where I can truly change lives.

I believe we all have the ability to tap into universal wisdom, collective consciousness, ancient wisdom; whatever you want to call it, through meditation, as part of our connection to what I call Source or our Higher Self. When one person thinks another person has "a problem," they aren't looking at the correct root of the problem. They are looking at that other person's controlling behavior. Once you realize that *you* are the root of your problem, then you have the power to correct it. As long as I think the other person is my problem, then I can't correct it. I have to get to *my* core issue and take a look to see what my energy is connected to. Am I feeling rejected? Why am I in denial? Why am I resistant? I look at my own problem to see that the other person is a reflection of it. We mirror each other's vibration.

A few years ago, a mother asked me if I would talk to her son. He had tried three times to commit suicide. The mom said he was a good kid, good grades, etc. Here comes this boy, absolutely gorgeous, about seventeen years old, and single.

During the reading, I saw an empty space. I asked, "Tell me about your dad."

He replied, "I don't know him. My mother got pregnant, and I never met my dad. I have no idea who he is."

Because he was a male, he needed the male energy that he didn't have. He was born with only female energy—which is emotions. So, if life got rough for him, he had no male strength to handle it, only emotional strength. He was totally out of balance energetically, and as a result was suicidal.

He sat with me and cried, "It makes so much sense now. Nobody has ever talked to me this way." I am convinced that children who are raised in a home with both mother and father or a strong balance of male and female energy will be more balanced themselves. A single mother who possesses both types of energy can achieve balance for the child, too.

The thing is, I am aware of the fact that I can affect a persons' energy and life—I can help them shift their consciousness. With the wisdom I receive, I can actually help change a persons' perspective. It is not only the words, but the feeling that backs up those words. I can feel the person lightening up as we share our vibration. When we vibrate at our highest level, we will feel joy. I had a client who came to see me about once a year. He said, "I don't get very much out of your readings, but I feel so damn good when I leave." That was him feeling our giving and receiving of energy. We balanced as one.

Energy embeds itself. Every item you own contains your energy. When I go in to clear a house, I can feel the energy. A happy family makes a happy house. I get the same senses about bodies: a body is happy or a body is sad. A body houses the spirit and all that a person has experienced. Houses hold memory, too, similar to muscle memory. In order to clear a house, I have to crack the energy. I can't just use a candle. Instead, I use sage. The smell shifts the vibration and stimulates the senses. Then I use salt to neutralize the energy, and I use loud, heavy-sounding bells to crack the energy. Recently I went to a house to clear it, and when I walked in, I had to take a breath, the feeling was that oppressive and heavy.

In another house, a woman witnessed a female entity walking through, and she thought it was terrifying her cute little scruffy mixed-breed dogs. The dogs had been barking more than usual, though when they growled and barked, the woman saw nothing there. An entity can choose whether or not to materialize—and when. The dogs sensed it. I was called in to clear the dense energy. I decided to use this opportunity to teach a class about house clearing and one of the students who came with me was a young woman, Sarah Yosick, an animal communicator who worked out of the Benicia psychic store I mentioned earlier—Angel Heart 4 You. Sarah was there to help protect the dogs. She crated them in a back room to keep them safe during the cleansing. The large Tibetan bell I use is loud, and we thought it might truly scare them.

Inside the house, the energy felt depressed, dense energy weighted the air. Remember, feelings are energy. You know how you can tell when your spouse or kids are happy or sad? You are feeling their vibration, whether it is dense or light. The dogs had been quiet, not a peep. As I got started and the vibration started breaking apart, a loud chilling scream that sounded like a woman in pain came from the back of the house. We all ran back there, but Sarah reached the crate first. She was shocked. The scream had come from one of the little dogs. Sarah fell down on her knees and lifted the crate. The scream was so piercing, she thought the dog had caught a toe or nail. Nothing was caught. The scream had come from the little dog, and it screamed into Sarah's face two more times, then stopped, and barked once. She stayed with the dogs, and they calmed as I continued clearing the house. The entity had entered the dog and screamed because of what I was doing. By the time we left, both dogs were fine—and relieved, I'm sure. An entity cannot be forced to depart. They stay as long as they choose. Usually they are attached to an article in the house, and if that attachment is severed, they choose to go to the light. I was never called back to that house.

At another house I was clearing, a papier mâché mask hung on the kitchen wall. I took one look at it and told the woman she did not want this on her wall. The mask was hideous, and being near it felt awful. The woman came in the room and looked shocked.

She had recently made the mask, starting with an impression of her own face, but now it did not look like her! Not even close! In a short period of time, whatever was in her home had attached itself to the mask. I finished clearing the house and went back to the kitchen—only to see that the mask once again had switched back and now resembled her attractive face again.

I had another call to clear a house. Upon arrival, I noted the staircase going up through the middle of the structure. The people who lived in the house had been feeling a coldness in one spot on the stairs. She was on the top step, and she looked like an old lady. I told everyone to stay back as I walked up to her. I climbed the stairs, feeling the circle of energy around this entity, and then I could see her in my mind. I asked her why she was here, and she said, "I am looking for my son." Immediately, I heard that her son had gone toward the light, and she only needed to reach out her hand because his was extended to her. She reached out her hand, and I experienced a blast of cold. When his hand took hers, the temperature began to rise. All of us in the room felt the warmth, and I saw them lift. I feel grateful to be able help not only living people but the people who need help crossing over.

• • •

We raise our own energy by connecting to Source through meditation, quiet, rest, and mostly through good, positive thoughts. If your energy is low, the best thing to do is rest and drink water. We can raise others' energy by acknowledging them or loving them. A caring touch near their heart or a hug will do the job, too. Or, try lowering your eyes, looking at their feet, while thinking about raising their energy, sending complementary messages such as, "You are beautiful, strong, loveable, valuable, etc." Then, slowly sweep your eyes up to the top of their head. Take a breath, exhale. You can do this without the other person knowing what you are doing. For instance, on those days when your husband is being a grouch, just raise his energy!

Think of yourself as pure energy with an energy force around you. When you think good things, the energy force speeds up. Conversely, bad thoughts slow the energy force down. Low energy can feel evil. It isn't evil, just low. I once was called to clear a house of "evil energy." The filth was hard to witness. The kitchen and living room were filled with dirty dishes. Cobwebs, black with dirt, hung from the ceiling in the teenagers' bedrooms and skimmed across my head. I had never seen such filth and disorganization, but it matched the low energy in the house. Dirtiness pulls on energy and lowers the energy of the people living in it. As I headed out the door, I told them to clean it up and then give me a call. Theirs was a physical problem as much as it was a spiritual problem.

Remember, love energy vibration is faster than fear or hate. If you have had a fight with another person, and you are really pissed off, that person didn't lower your energy, you did. Judgment lowers your energy and joy raises it. I could try to fluff up your energy for ten hours, but I would be of little help. We are totally in control of our own energy. In my classes I have demonstrated fluffing up energy by taking my hands and making an upward fluffing motion all around a person. I ask him or her to think negative thoughts—sad thoughts. As soon as they do, their energy goes down—they can feel the change against my fluffing—and they learn that they are in total control of their energy thermostat, no one else. In this lifetime, we are here to learn how to keep this energy up. We lower and raise it in response to love and fear. Yet one more big learning curve. The key is to know that nobody is doing anything *to* us—we are in control. If you don't like me and that lowers my energy, I am not in charge of myself. If you tell me I'm a bitch, and I KNOW I'm not a bitch, you are not going to lower my energy. When you reach the point that no one else can bring down your energy, you are empowered in all avenues of your life.

A woman came to see me. She had rheumatoid arthritis and a tremendous amount of guilt around her mother's passing, which had happened about a year before our meeting. When I asked how long she had suffered from arthritis, she said, "About a year."

I said to her, "Because of your guilt, you took on your mother's pain."

My job, then, was to work on her feelings of guilt and help her forgive herself.

When what bothers us is allowed to eat away at us for long enough, cancer arises. Deep hurt or secret unresolved feelings develop into a *"what's the use"* attitude and is the inner turmoil cancer preys upon. When I was a child, I was abused. When I was thirty, I had a cancerous uterus removed. I know there was a connection.

Before the surgery, a friend called. I hadn't seen this friend for several weeks. She said, "I wanted to tell you I had a hysterectomy. I had cancer of the uterus."

I told her that I hadn't had a check-up in a long time. This conversation kicked me into gear, and I went for an exam. I had cancer of the uterus. Her call was not an accident or coincidence, and as is usually the case with uterine cancer, I had no symptoms. That call saved my life in more than one way. The surgery cut out the rage I held toward the abuse. My friend had been abused also, and she instinctively knew they were cutting the abuser out.

I started having panic attacks three months after my father died. To the little girl in me, his death was the ultimate abandonment. When I was having these attacks, a woman who was a counselor of some type came to me for a reading. When we were done, I said, "I might have to come see you because I have panic attacks."

Just off the cuff, she said, "Use your father's name."

"Why did you say that?" I asked.

"Well, I don't tell people, but I am a little bit of a channel and, I just heard 'Use your father's name.'"

This was interesting because I had never used my father's name, Castro. As I was raised by my stepfather—who I hated—I always used his surname, Rafael. I started to change my name everywhere I could. I was now Connie Castro Jackson. I had been plagued by fear and unable to talk in front of people up until then. After changing my name, the first time after I started to talk in front of a group. I said, "My name is Connie Castro," and I waited for that panic to start taking over ". . . Jackson." Oh my God, no panic! I have a belief that we are not complete until we walk with the energy of our beginnings—our mother and father. I have to have the power of both. I think the panic my body held all my life was fear of abandonment. What if people find out I am uneducated and poor? I won't measure up, and they might abandon me.

This is how I learned about the energetic power in a name. People who use a nickname frequently aren't functioning under full power, unless that nickname has more power. Many people I read for change their names, especially if they have been abused. That childhood energy may have a name attached to it doesn't work anymore. One client of mine faced the fact that she had been abused as a child, and when this memory resurfaced, she changed her name and found herself more powerful. Such sadness was attached to her childhood name, she couldn't shake the sadness until she changed what she called herself.

You can test the resistance in a name by using muscle testing. Have the person being tested stand in front of you and clasp their hands together, holding them out perpendicular to their body. Tell them to say their name three times. Then, they must try to resist as you pull down on their clasped hands. If the hands are easy to pull down, the name has no power. If you feel resistance (hard for you to pull their hands down) when they say their name, the name does hold power. One of my clients is six feet, five inches tall, and, of course, I am five feet, one inch on a good day. He was unable to resist my pulling when he said his childhood name. But when he tried using an adult name he preferred, I was not able to pull down his arms.

I was talking to a woman the other day. The two of us were on completely different vibrational levels. She said she was mad at her son because he'd "gotten his girlfriend pregnant." She was angry, and all I could think of was that she was setting up resistance, not only with her son but with this unborn child.

I said to her, "Why not just love this baby? The fact is, she is pregnant. There is nothing you can do about it. You have the choice to set up resistance with the child or you can love the child. You are already sharing energy with this child and you are sharing it with your son and his girlfriend."

She looked at me like I was nuts.

This is what is interesting. It goes back to our beginnings. She said she had been talking to her mother and her sisters and everyone was upset. I said, "That's because they got the information from you! Had you called them and said 'Guess what, I am so excited, we are having a baby, and I'm going to be a grandma,' they would have taken it differently."

I truly believe that our lessons start in the womb, and that she was setting up a pattern of rejection for a person's life and distance in her relationship with a grandchild. Her vibration was one of judgment toward a baby who, sadly, would experience as his or her first disappointment the feeling of being unwanted by her.

I am certain that I was resistant to being dark-skinned even before I was born. I never wanted to be out in the sun and was obsessed with not getting any darker. During my time in the womb, I shared blood with a woman who was embarrassed about being pregnant with a dark baby. My believe is that I *had* to feel that coming from her in order to understand that many lessons do begin in the womb. If you slap me, I will be mad, and I will know why I am mad. But if I experienced this trauma in the womb, before I had language for memories, I could be angry and frustrated but not remember why. Realizing this helped me understand why I was always mad at my mother. I had unconscious memory of not being wanted and that the resistance between us had been set before I was born. I craved her acknowledgment. Here she was, white as snow, unmarried, pregnant for the sixth time—and with a dark baby in the highly prejudicial era of the 1930s. I know how hard her life was for her, and I understand what it feels like to be judged by people. I have to say, that woman worked every day to take care of us. She loved us and spent her life working to provide for us. Understanding why I felt resistance toward her lightened my load and gave me peace.

When we are stuck in old patterns of victimhood, we draw the same situations to ourselves again and again. In his book, *The Power of Now*, Eckhart Tolle says, "We can shift the energy of victimhood that perpetuates our old problems by becoming aware of our own power in the present. A victim identity is the belief that the past is more powerful than the present, which is the opposite of the truth. It is the belief that other people and what they did to you are responsible for who you are now, for your emotional pain or your inability to be your true self. The truth is that the only power there is, is contained within this moment. Once you know that, you realize you are responsible for your own inner peace now—nobody else is, and that the past cannot prevail against the power of the Now."

• • •

Let me tell you a story of lessons being set up very early.

A woman came for a reading. She was distraught about her daughter who had been adopted from a Russian orphanage. The couple wanted a child to love, but the girl had been raised in a baby bed, hardly held or cared for until she was adopted at three years old. She had never been let out of the crib; she couldn't walk or talk. She understood a little Russian, but couldn't speak it. Coming back from Russia was awful, she screamed all the way on the plane. The child was mean, vicious even, spitting at her adoptive parents, trying to hurt them. She was more than they could handle. And she was terribly afraid.

The couple had been parents for almost a year. In my reading I saw the little girl flying through the air. I described this to the mom, and she was embarrassed to admit, "I threw her one day. I had just had it with her, and I threw her. She came up and bit me and I just reacted."

They were going to take her back to Russia. As I understand it, if the adoption isn't working out the parents have a year to take a kid back. They didn't want to, but they didn't know what else to do.

I centered and connected with the little girl. Usually when I connect with someone, I perceive two distinct sides of their personality; fear and love. With this little girl, there was no love side. All was fear. She was full of fear, frustration, and anger. Never having been taught to talk or walk, she was much like an abused animal. Love was never programmed in for this girl. In order for her to learn to cope with life, they would have to program in love. They would have to treat her like a newborn and simply love her. There could be no reprimanding. Even if she misbehaved, they must do nothing but love her.

She was never returned to Russia, and it has been more than fifteen years. The family moved to another state, but I have heard that she is doing well. She gets good grades in school and is quite the gymnast. She is not very affectionate with her parents but is with her brother.

Programming love can be so easy. I saw the Dalai Lama, the exiled Tibetan Buddhist Monk, whose wisdom is so simple. He was asked "How do you practice compassion?" The Dalai looked at the man with a smile on his face and said "Well, you could be nice." He has such a warm and sweet sense of humor.

Thich Nhat Hanh, a Vietnamese Buddhist Monk, is a little man who looks so much like my dad that I fell in love with him. He talked quietly at a gathering of about a thousand people, still we could hear every word he said, people were that respectful and quiet. His message about love was, "You must love your children. Let me show you how to love your children." About ten children sat near him. He walked over to each and hugged them. He turned to the audience and said, "That's the way you love your children." His magical way is to make everything simple.

I am seeing young girls come in for readings, and I am surprised at their wisdom. I didn't know I had wisdom at their age. At each change in perspective, I have felt my wisdom grow, but this has taken years. Like going to school, you learn how to do math, then you learn to do bigger math problems, but it is still math. Recently, it seems to me that the human race is evolving at a faster pace. Kids are becoming more aware, and many of them are Indigo kids. Indigos are wiser at an earlier age; their launching pads start at a higher level. A teacher and counselor, Nancy Ann Tapp, studied human auras (electromagnetic fields) and saw that eighty percent of kids she studied who were born after 1980 had "indigo" blue auras. Other researchers noted that these kids come in to this lifetime with an inner knowing. Some say they think the human brain waves are moving toward higher vibrations. A few of the attributes of an Indigo is that they have more confidence, know they belong, find many rules silly, are insightful, strong willed, think-out-of-the-box creative, are easily bored, intuitive or psychic. I think we all know young people who fit the description. Indigos are becoming harder to contain in a classroom and to parent. We have to take a look at shifting the paradigms both at home and in our schools.

My Deborah was an example of the child teaching the mother, with awareness beyond her age. As a little girl, she was naturally compassionate beyond her years. She was always acknowledged in her life, so she had little resistance and was able to show her gifts, her love. She could see things at an early age that even I hadn't figured out yet. Interesting to note, my mother and I did not get along, but because my daughter Deborah was her love, I felt that my mother and I loved each other through her. She became the energy, the vibration of love, that connected us.

I feel that the universe can only give to us what we vibrate. If I send out a vibration, a thought, to the Universe that I hate gambling or gamblers, either or both will show up in my life. I need to learn to stop hating gamblers. Dislike is a stronger vibration than like. Words and thoughts are so strong, they come in loud and clear to the universe. The universe does not distinguish between dislike and like, so be careful. If I think I don't like gamblers, the universe hears only my vibrational thought . . . gamblers.

Addiction is a strong vibrational thought. I believe we all have addictions of one kind or another. I have come to recognize my mine as the need to be loved, and I think many of us are the same. Such addictions are not visible; they go unseen. Most of us wouldn't recognize our habits of thought as addiction. When we have a problem, and we can't see a label to make it obvious, we need to dig in and find it. People will appear in our lives who show by example what we need to learn and what our addictive need looks like. They aren't there just to annoy us. Since I have the need to be loved, I will find similar people coming into my life. Watch for similar patterns in your own life.

In order to get away from an addiction, you have to become a part of it. I wanted to be loved in a family but if I wasn't feeling the love, I felt slighted and would push myself out by feeling hurt and getting quiet. I needed to change that, to stop stepping outside and do whatever I needed to in order to join in and become a part of the family. I had to learn how to love. I had to learn that we get what we give.

As a child, I would be naughty to get attention. I got my fix, and then I was satisfied. Love feels like fullness. When we aren't feeling loved, we feel empty. Food, alcohol, drug addictions, and the need to please all have at their root the need to be loved. As soon as I don't feel loved, I feel empty. I have to fill the void—eat too may chocolates, belt down too many martinis, and so on. All the time searching for those loving arms, and the path to finding that full, peaceful feeling of sharing loving energy, which is unique for each of us.

BECOME YOUR POWER

Emotional fears such as rejection and failure, are like the petals of rose. We must peel back the layers of these emotions to get at the center, the core of what's causing them. When the petals of a rose are closed, we can't see the full beauty of the rose or completely experience its sweetness. Humans are the same. In order to grow and expand, to glimpse how unique we each are as a spiritual being, we must peel back and open our petals by sharing our beliefs with others.

Life is school, but it is also a rehab center. We all have addictive personalities. We are addicted to whatever causes us pain. We come into this "rehab" to explore these addictions. Until we get to the core cause, we cannot heal. Alcohol, drugs, etc., are physical addictions, easy to pinpoint because they are the ones we can see. Emotional addictions are lessons that walk beside us invisibly. We can't see them, but we sure can feel them.

The long road requires us to acknowledge the perfection in who we are and what we are, and the only way I can be perfect is to allow you to be perfect. We can't exist within our own power until we accept perfection in others and allow the world to be as it is without trying to change it. Until we understand that, we can't love fully, because we can't love and judge at the same time.

We become addicted to the *feeling of needing to be loved*, which is a form of pain. I had struggled with this most of my life, until I recognized that *I am my own energy generator*. This is the sensation we are all grabbing for. I don't need to be loved by you if I love myself, which is what happens when I stop judging myself. Learning to generate our own energy is a major life lesson and a hard one to master. Even now, at times I find myself looking to others to be my energy generator.

Knowing comes in levels, or dimensions, and as I've said, is a lifelong process. We are peeling back the addictions and the fears to find the sweetness who is God, Higher Self, Spirit, or Source. As we gain wisdom, we move into different levels of awareness or dimensions. Each of us is wise. No one is higher or more important than another, but we shift gears at different times, into a different direction or area of growth. A few years back, I had mastered several levels, but now I can see from a new perspective, an even higher or deeper truth. I realize that compassion is all encompassing. It is not just for the poor and needy but also for people I don't agree with or who don't have the same needs as I do. We each have a unique view of what life is about, and as we grow in wisdom, our perceptions change uniquely, too.

Relationships with people are the primary reflection of who we are and are our most constant teachers. Know also that we are reflected in our relationships to animals, events, places. These mirror our choices, feelings, and the value that we place on ourselves.

We constantly grow and change, and these changes don't always feel good. Our relationship with ourselves sets the tone for relationships with others. It is a constant back and forth balancing act and must be tended to as a priority. A problem with another person indicates an imbalance within you. The word imbalance is not the ideal word to describe what is going on within you when you feel unwell physically or mentally. What is perceived as imbalance is the body balancing itself in response to your thoughts. All is in balance at all times, but when the mind and body do not register harmoniously and these conditions are not tended to by you in a way that allows relief and better feelings, you won't feel clear. Your thoughts and physical body will feel muddled. Harmony must be created and nurtured within ourselves before we can expect a relationship with another to provide us with a sense of pleasure and fulfillment.

I have mentioned that our children are our greatest teachers, and they are: they reflect us back to ourselves. My daughter Deborah and I were going to see the Dalai Lama. I had planned on it being a special time for the two of us, but I never mentioned it. She called, saying her friend was coming along, never giving thought to the possibility that I might want time alone with her. When she wanted to share the event with a friend, I was pissed all day, felt totally rejected.

I eventually realized it was my fault for not being clear. I should have said something. Instead, I spent the day focused on the pain of rejection and not the wonderful time to be had. Nor did I pay attention to how considerate my daughter was to think of sharing with her friend. And my sweet little stepdaughters—it took me years to realize what a gift they are. I had a stepfather I hated and was given stepdaughters I learned to love very much, and I was able to transcend those painful, negative emotions.

If it is your goal to have peaceful, passionate, joyous, loving connections with family and friends, you must begin with yourself wherever you are now and take responsibility not only for your feelings but your commitment to a happy self. Though you may imagine that others are taking care of you or holding you back or moving you forward or taking advantage of you, in actuality they are mirroring your relationship to yourself, which is, in fact, the most valuable gift they could give you.

Source is within, and if you think of yourself as separate from Source you will have no power. Thoughts hold tremendous power. As long as my thoughts are peaceful, I am maintaining my connection with Source. When I am anything but peaceful, I lose energy. Stay in peace and life is given to us. Our humanness interrupts the flow. Turn on your energy by loving someone.

Again, we receive what we give. This is the sweetness and grace that brings peace.

• • •

Meditation puts us into the eye the hurricane. It turns our focus from outside to in. For most of us in the U.S., life is spent looking at the outside, reacting. The meditative state resides in that quiet place where we connect with Source and its powerful energy. We do this by stilling our minds.

I have heard many times, "I can't meditate, my mind keeps wandering!" Yes, you can, you just don't know it yet. When your mind wanders off from the meditative word or breath, or mantra you are using, allow it to do so, and then gently bring your focus back in. You can meditate with music, breathing, repeating a mantra, walking while focusing on pebbles—many ways are available to us. As many ways as there are personalities. A number of people find they center themselves better with mantras like "OOHHMM" or similar vocal sounds, others like guided meditation. I prefer soft music and the sound of my breath. In that meditative place is where you sense oneness with yourself, your highest self, that which we call Source or God. Have you ever been driving a car and missed a familiar turnoff? You were somewhere else. You had gone inward. Certain songs or melodies can take us to that place. Betty Bethards used to meditate to Elvis Presley. In some of her lectures she would play Elvis! Meditating is quieting the mind, stopping the chatter and worry, using whatever it takes. Please know that we all have to practice staying in the meditative state, and it is common for thoughts to wander.

Thich Nhat Hanh, the Nobel Peace Prize winner, Vietnamese Zen Master, and Buddhist monk said, "When you eat, eat. When you read, read."

A person in his audience said, "But Mr. Hanh, I saw you eating *and* reading the other day."

He replied, "When you eat and read, eat and read."

Be in that moment, whatever that moment is. Total focus without outside influence.

During one meditation session, I experienced an awakening. I saw myself sitting under a tree at a beach. A sad woman walked toward me and asked me to help her. I gave her advice as she told her story. When we finished talking, she walked away, and I began to cry: I realized she was me. Source brought to my imagination a symbol I could connect with. A rare thing. But I was disconnected enough from the world to receive and understand the message intended for me.

My best meditation times are when I let my imagination go free, forgetting about my surroundings. I am able to connect with and talk to Source and to ask questions. When a symbol comes into your meditation, a person, an animal, a tree—anything—try talking to it, in your imagination, and listen quietly to what it has to say. Messages come to us in different ways. For beginners; be very present with and aware of the thoughts that come to you and write them down. Symbols are important and are the same as dream symbols. After all, how do we know if we are awake or asleep?

Most people think that the purpose of meditation is to handle stress, to tune out, to get away from it all. While that's partially true, the real purpose of meditation is to *tune in,* not to escape but to get in touch, not to de-stress but to find the peace within that we hear so much about. The peace that spiritual traditions describe as surpassing all understanding. In other words, meditation is a way to get into the space between your thoughts. You have a thought here and a thought there, with little space between each thought. This space between thoughts is the window, the corridor, the vortex to the infinite mind. It is the mystery that people call the spirit or God. We don't have to use those terms. We can call it core consciousness. Either way, the more we learn about this space between thoughts, the closer we get to the absolute truth of self. Truth is a field of infinite possibility and pure potentiality and the reality that everything is connected to everything else, a place of infinite creativity and the infinite power of intention.

To sum it up—through meditation, you can reach your highest level of consciousness, beyond your emotional and physical realities, and gain a greater understanding of your life's lessons. You learn to process emotional and physical experience through higher levels of awareness. You see that none of us is here to judge another's journey, only to witness what needs to be cleansed in ourselves. Remember, judgment creates resistance, which blocks your energy source and creates karma. We can all learn to exist as our higher selves in everyday life. You know when you are there when you feel peace. Meanwhile, Ego is the enemy of peace. Shut that fear voice down, or IT WILL TELL YOU THAT YOU CAN'T.

Beware, as undesirable entities exist and need to be recognized and avoided. I will share some experiences. Helga was a trans-channel. This is a spirit who comes through another person. Vern Bronson moved to Benicia and moved in with a friend of mine, Elsie. Elsie was highly spiritual, quite controlling, and the biggest bitch in town; but at the same time very kind. Vern, having just moved up from Southern California, rented a room from her. He had owned ice cream parlors, got tired of the life, and came north. He happened to move in with hyper-spiritual Elsie. At the time I was doing her hair, and she recommended me to him as a hairstylist, so that's how we met.

One day he told Elsie he had begun hearing a voice. After explaining to him what I do other than hairdos, she suggested he talk to me about it. I invited Vern to our house that night. Ray thought I was nuts, certain once again that I was bringing crazy people into the house.

Vern came over and told me that this voice calls herself Helga.

Once she started coming through, I could detect the difference in their voice patterns. He talked slowly, and Helga talked fast, with a sharp edge. I asked her why she chose Vern and she said, "Why not?" She was good about answering a number of questions, but then things went haywire. The information coming through grew crazy and couldn't be trusted, so Vern just stopped. He was embarrassed.

However, he let me set him up to do a few groups, and he enjoyed it. But, one night the group got angry with him—actually with Helga, but Vern was their target. The audience cussed him out. He was almost sick over it. The week before, one of the women in the group had asked Helga a question, and Helga's answer was, "If you go down to Benicia to the end of First Street at 7:30, you will meet an alien." The woman went! Vern was embarrassed enough that he never did it again. He moved out of state, but years later he came back to visit, and we had coffee. He said he never brought up Helga again. Just because a channeled entity is a spirit, doesn't mean they have more wisdom than the person channeling. I felt Helga was toying with Vern. I know it was no accident or coincidence that Vern and I met so I could help him through this connection.

• • •

It is important to know also that we can create circumstances we don't want if worry becomes a prayer. The Universe hears only our thoughts such as "I want someone to come into my life to love me." If our thoughts are "I don't want someone who is older, short, and poor," the Universe will hear only the description and guess what, old, short, poor guys will show up. The "I don't want" part isn't understood. Put thoughts out to the Universe that are clearly what you want, not what you don't want. If prayer is an intention that we announce to the universe in order to create a desired outcome, then our every thought is a prayer. This includes thoughts of worry as well as of hope. All thoughts are subtle creative energy. Some are more focused or repeated more often, gathering strength. Some are written down or spoken, giving them even greater power. Every thought we have is a part of a process whereby we co-create our experience and our reality with the universe. When we use our creative energy unconsciously, we create what is commonly known as a self-fulfilling prophecy. When we worry, we are repeatedly praying and lending our energy to the creation of realities we don't want.

The good news is that we can retrain our minds and thoughts to focus our energy on what we do desire to bring into our lives. Since worry is often repetitive, it takes more than one positive thought to counteract the energy we have created. The simplest antidote to worry is affirmation. Repeat positive thoughts often, speak and write them and refer to them throughout the day, using focused energy to create positive results.

Start now with this thought:

I am a creative being, using my energy to co-create a wonderful world. I create my experience of life from within, and as I do so, I create ripples of energy around me, which echo into the world. My positive thought combines with thought and prayers of others. Together we create positive energy enough to heal not only our own lives but the world we share. I am grateful for the ability to co-create good in my life and the world.

When concerned loved ones worry about us, they are sending out a worry prayer to the world. Worry never did anybody any good. Explain to your worrier in a loving conversation that wishing for good things is much more beneficial. Ask them to send positive affirmations rather than worrying about you. For example, *I know Charlotte will get that job if it is the right one for her*, rather than *I am so scared Charlotte won't get that job, and then what will she do?*

In this lifetime, I channel higher wisdom, but my purpose is love and compassion. Every human's truth is love and compassion, but at times we need to be reminded. When I need to connect to Source, I meditate. I ask the Light of love and compassion to fill and surround me, let their wisdom to come through me, and for Guidance to guide me. I end with "I am blessed" three times and "namaste" because I do honor my guides as I do myself. It took years of practice for me to get centered and recognize the feeling of being connected to Source.

A burning bowl is another way to connect to source. You write down your intention, stand in a circle around the bowl with burning sage (we burn sage because it cleanses) and then drop the notes with intentions into the fire. The first time I did this, when the smoke started coming out of the bowl, things felt different. The smoke resembled an arm, and as we watched, curled toward a particular person, then curled back and over to cleanse the next person on the right, and so on, in order. One by one, the twelve of us were cleansed as the smoke went back into the bowl and out again to each of us, completing the circle twice. No one spoke. No breeze or air moved. We had been addressing Source with our intentions to make positive changes in our lives, and we were being shown, at our individual levels of enlightenment, that more is happening here than we think.

I start the burning bowl, saying to the group, "Tonight we will use the burning bowl, each of us in turn, to ask that the behavioral patterns that keep us from experiencing our truths and higher selves be released. Let these thoughts and feelings come to mind so you can turn them to ash and release." The ashes represent anxiety, insecurity, guilt, fear, envy, worry, procrastination, impatience, blame, indecision, rejection, judgment, frustration, need for approval, etc. When everyone present has written their intentions on a slip of paper, I ask them to come to the bowl, one at a time, to place their paper in their fire, intensifying the intention by saying, **"I turn you to ashes, I am free."** When Source understands clearly what we are working on manifesting, the help will be there.

In a reading, if I tap into your vibration of love and compassion, you will hear me. You feel Source, but you will hear me—but if and only if we connect vibrationally. At that point, our vibrations have equalized, bringing that sense of peace. First, I acknowledge your strengths but not your problem. If I started with, "You are jealous. This is your fault," I would be matching your lowest vibration, the one you came here to fix. I have to raise your vibration by getting you to acknowledge what your truth is. Whatever you are struggling with has nothing to do with who you are. You are a loving, compassionate being. The other stuff, the problems or issues, is what you yourself have tacked on. With the wisdom that comes from Source through me, I can help you change your life by shifting your conscious perspective. I am aware of this. I also understand that it is the feeling behind the words, not the words alone, that bring this about.

I sense a person's energy lightening as I talk to them, as we move to share vibrational energy. A very depressed woman once told me that an odd thing happened when she passed a streetlight. The light dimmed or went out. Of course! She was draining the energy! As I keep repeating, we are only here to learn, and if I want to learn, I need to be in the flow of peace. Remember, judgment limits flow. If I attach a label, then I limit my flow. Never forget we are not only a body. We are spirit, too. In order to stay in peace, I have to be aware that I am the creator, the director, and also the resistor of my spiritual flow.

• • •

During a connection with Source, I asked, "Who are you?"

The voice said, "I am everyone."

I asked, "Why do humans have to suffer?" and was told, "Humans don't have to suffer, it is a choice. There are those who struggle because that is a way. There are those who struggle because they see it as a challenge."

I asked, "Why don't we all see the same?"

I was told, "The stories began before entering life. You who are learning about love and compassion will limit your view depending upon your own sadness. True compassion is the all, not just the human standing on the corner, hungry. Every human is hungry. Every human struggles. Every human feels pain until they see God or the Source."

If I think my way is the only way, then I am limiting myself. If I can allow myself to believe that *every way is the way*, then I broaden my energy field. I don't have a plan because I don't know what the plan is. The Christians, the Buddhists or Muslims, they all have a plan—and look what happens. Now they are all fighting to have their way be "THE WAY." People hand their power over to their belief system. I don't like having a middleman.

I came into my current reality as a highly intuitive individual. As I grew, I questioned the unknown and became curious about it. So, the unknown was fed back to me. Information is given to us in our "own language." I know that my life was presented to me by the wisdom of Source, because it was the life I needed to experience. Why did I see spirits as a child when other people didn't? Why are Pentecostals able to speak in tongues or Catholics perform exorcisms, and I can't? Why do I look the way I look? Why do you look the way you look? Why are you the way you are? Why do you think the way you think? What are the recurring parallels in your life? When you start asking yourself these questions, you begin to recognize that your purpose is what you learn as you journey toward the answers. It resides in the lessons appearing along the way.

Learn to use what you are born with. You are born with all different types and quantities of wisdom, different dimensions, learning styles and abilities, types of intelligence, karma, and experiences in the womb. You just have to awaken to it. I can channel all day, but do math or use technology—no way!

• • •

You might remember that Betty Bethards said, "As we grow spiritually, our eyes change." The light begins to come on, and it shows through our eyes. They shine with specks or sparkles of light and might appear lighter in color. But in your life, in your day-to-day, not much changes.

For instance, you might still have the fear of rejection or of being alone. Nothing has changed because the fears are still there. They've lost part of their bite as you have grown spiritually, but they still have a presence. I recognize I have grown because they don't affect me in the same way as they did when I was less experienced. Always, however, just when I thought I had the answers, the questions got bigger, went deeper.

The journey and the destination are one, traveled by the body, the mind, and the spirit combined. My journey is to find out who I am. I have to fight all of my battles in order to reach the point of recognizing myself, and they must be fought in a loving way. If I fight with fear, I will get out of my flow. Put another way, as Guidance has told me, we are put on this earth to find our way home and the only weapon we are given is love.

I believe there is nothing in life to be feared, only understood. Fear will block wisdom.

I've mentioned that when Ray and I moved to Benicia, years ago, I started having panic attacks. In Stockton, I was around friends and family, and I was successful because I was in my element. When we moved, I couldn't even say my name in front of a group of new people. This was a shock because in Stockton I had lead groups and classes with no problem. I went to a class just after I arrived in Benicia, and when it was my turn to introduce myself, my body tensed. I could barely talk, let alone say my name, the pressure in my chest was so intense. I joined Toastmasters to see if I could conquer this fear. In fact, I tried everything I could think of.

Now, let me tell you how guidance works. I got a phone call from a woman, Elizabeth Caulder—I will never forget her. I thought she was calling about the phone readings I was doing at the time. She said, "Connie, I am a producer, and how would you like to go on radio or TV?" A friend of hers had been in Benicia visiting his family, and he had come to me for a reading. He played the tape of my reading for her, and she was impressed.

As soon as she spoke, I experienced a panic attack so severe I could hardly breathe. I said as calmly as possible, "Elizabeth, can I call you back?"

So many times, I said no to things because I was shy. I didn't have panic attacks in Stockton, but I was still shy. When I was asked to do something, if I felt afraid, I said I was too busy, or had to take the kids to school, or had to fix dinner. I blamed others for my shyness. When I called Elizabeth back and for the first time was honest about the panic, I felt wonderful. I said, "Elizabeth I have panic attacks. I really do want to go on radio but I cannot go on TV."

She said, "Just let me know when you are ready."

It turned out to be about a year later. During that year, she called once a month and said, "Connie, how are you doing. Are you ready?"

I would say, "Not yet."

She was okay with that. After a few months, she called and said she didn't know why she kept calling me. When people aren't interested, she usually stopped calling. I knew why. She was an angel for me, and she was helping me learn how to speak and share myself. I made a promise to myself to go for it. It wasn't about being famous, but about doing it and not dying.

I finally called Elizabeth to say go, and she put me on the radio in Las Vegas. I talked from my house, though the callers called in from different places to ask questions. I felt terrified. I was right on target with my answer to the first caller's question, something about his wife.

Right on the radio he said, "I have never talked to anyone who could give me an answer about this. My God, you are wonderful, just fantastic." And so on.

Now, hey! That was an angel because I did the rest of the hour, and I *was* wonderful. During my next stint, I was hooked up to a caller in Kansas, and boy did I get it. This guy called from a pay phone (no cell phones then) and said, "I am so angry, so very angry that they would allow a person like you to be on the radio. I am just furious. Do you realize that this is devil's work and do you know that this is possession?" He was giving me the riot act over the phone and I started to panic. I wanted to hang up that phone so badly, and I could have, but I had committed myself to this and I would see it through. I don't remember what I said to him, exactly, probably nothing brilliant, but this prepared me for confrontations with people like him. The next time I went on the radio, I had my notes in front of me—the definition of a dream, a channel etc. That helped, and my confidence grew. Elizabeth put me on six times that year, then I never heard from her again. It was done. I had learned my lesson, and my angel had set me up well.

Throughout my life, whenever I needed to have confidence, to feel good about myself, an angel has shown up. Once, I was talking in front of a forty-person audience, and I thought I was awful. I was so nervous my thoughts were scrambled. As I left the stage with my tail between my legs, certain I had bombed, a woman approached, saying how good I was. She said she wished she could express herself as well as I did. I felt ready to try again. When I acknowledged the fear, I saw I had been hiding the fact that I had felt stupid most of my life. My lack of education was complicated by some kind of learning disability that makes me need to visualize what is written in order to understand it. I have to go over a piece of writing several times before I can retain it.

Then there was my lack of vocabulary. Fear is such a block. Fear thrusts us backward, splitting us into separate components, taking us off the path while we deal with it.

As disabling as fear can be, I believe it is a choice.

We create fear; it can't exist on its own. It is a state of mind we create and create from. Fear comes in many levels, and without it, we couldn't learn—it is a learning tool. We need to face it and see what the lesson is in order for it to go away. I believe that fear is not only a choice but the absence of Source energy. Choosing peace over fear takes a lifetime of learning. Source is the real true you, and connecting to it is like turning on the headlights so you can see around you while driving. The lights are not *keeping* you safe, they are *showing* you that you are safe. A child born into an environment of fear has easy access to it. Training themselves away from being fearful will be a major lifetime lesson on their paths.

Some thoughts:

You must stop taking credit or blame. Recognize that everyone is on their journey and, frankly it's none of your business to judge in any way.

One of my favorite quotes is by Terry Cole Whitacre: "It's none of my business what you think of me."

Others aren't judging you. You are judging you.

If you HAVE to be right, you are wrong.

You aren't here to please anyone, but to be pleasing to yourself.

• • •

When I first met Ray's family, I was a little stand-offish, uncomfortable being outside my circle. Then, look what happened—my daughter married a man who wanted nothing to do with us, and since my being born dark-skinned was my greatest disappointment, of course every boyfriend Deborah ever had was dark.

She came home one day talking about going to the prom, all excited. She started to say something, but then she said, "Oh Mom, I don't need to explain that to you, you aren't like other mothers."

"What?"

"Oh, never mind, you aren't going to care or be upset. You aren't like the other mothers."

"Deborah I am upset, tell me!"

"Well, my date is black."

I guess the look on my face was shock.

She started to cry and said "You are like everybody else."

Now, you have to understand I never have thought of myself as prejudiced, but I never wanted to be dark because to me that meant being poor. All from my experience in the womb. So, my karma was that my daughter would date only dark men and would marry a man from Lebanon. I can go back and show you every truth about myself I gathered along the way, all because in my mind I thought I had to be white to be successful. My perception was skewed.

I've said this, too: Deborah was special. I birthed an angel, and I think about that a lot. People asked me how I raised her, since she was so wonderful. I said I loved her and gave her anything she wanted. But she asked for nothing. When she was little, I would take her shopping and say, "How about this, Deborah?" and she asked how much it cost. "It doesn't matter how much," I would say. Her response was, "Shouldn't we ask Dad?" At Christmastime when she was five, she counted the gifts and there had better be the same number each for her and her sisters or we had to go shopping. She brought me balance and at a very early age taught me compassion. I think that's no accident or coincidence.

The thing is, this is all so simple. My past, present and future are one. I am still dealing with my past. I will always deal with my past. I know I still have fears. So, if I am dealing with my past, isn't this also my present—who I am now? Since I look toward my future and am still dealing with my distant past and present, isn't that my future? I was a young adult, now I am an old lady, but I am still that child. We three are one. I am still and always will be in correction and learning mode, finding my power in any new situation.

As we age, we can get stuck, however. I started doing hair the 1950s. I am talking pin curls! When Vidal Sassoon came on the scene and introduced style cutting in the '70s, we had to go back for training. Style cutting was cutting hair to be blown dry. Part of the training was about working with the middle-aged woman who has worn her hair long since she was a teen. She identifies with long hair because when she first wore it that way, she was happy. The long hair and the happiness were one. That woman will not change her hair until she makes changes in her awareness. The look of a woman's hair is an important part of her identity and affects how she feels about herself.

I'll give you an example. My little sister is a spitfire. She decided to become a beautician, too, and on her first day of work, a woman with curly hair came in for a cut. The woman was adamant that her bangs stay long. Nita had never cut such curly hair and didn't allow length enough for the bangs to spring back after they were cut. They shot up short! The woman was so stuck on how she wanted to look and so angry that she slapped Nita. Nita decked her, ending her career as a beautician. But, talk about power—that woman felt her power was in her hairdo.

Up until a few years ago I had a hard time staying alone. Always I have felt the sensation of *not* being alone, although I never could see who was there. I was afraid of being by myself because of it. Now I know those are my spirit guides. They walk with us every moment, but not everyone can feel their presence. I didn't understand this when I was young. Having my name called when nobody is there? So creepy.

I still hate being alone at night, but I have human angels: my daughters and friends who will come and stay if I need them. When Ray was still alive, if he was called out of town, I'd call Deborah, and she'd say, "Your house or mine." For a long time, I had no power over the fear.

At one point a male guide came in to my consciousness. Now, understand, this is taking place in my imagination. Imagination is a wonderful tool for us. One night, I dreamed this man was sitting on the side of my bed talking to me. He was a chubby little guy in a green polyester suit. He took me by the hand, and we walked into a toy store. My granddaughter, Josie, was little at the time, and she came into the dream. She and I walked hand in hand into the store. Sitting in the corner was a box with three wooden toy dogs inside. The little dogs jumped out and started walking toward us, but as they got closer, they began to get ferocious. In fact, they turned mean and evil and kept coming at us. I started to run with Josie. My guide took my hand, stopped me, looked me in the eyes, and said, "There is no fear." I pointed at the dogs and in my strongest voice I said, "Get back in the box!" They turned away and ran, and as they jumped back into the box, they became wooden toys again. From that point on, for years, the little chubby guy in green polyester was always with me during a reading.

That dream changed my life, and I will never forget it. I woke up certain that I had met my guide, and he was showing me my power—my power over fear. For as far back as I can remember, every six months or so, I would wake up in a state of total panic, terrified, feeling "IT" back in the room. Not too much later, one night I *thought* I was awake, feeling "IT" back again. The words *I am so tired of you* passed through my head. I grabbed the thing and started slinging. I could hear it hitting the walls, but I couldn't see it. The sound became less and less. When I realized I was still asleep, I forced myself to the surface, thinking, *Oh my God, I just did battle with my fear.* Later, I was getting centered for a reading, and a beautiful woman came floating in. I was a little resentful, and asked her who she was. She said she was my female guide. She sat on the other side from my little chubby guy. For many years, the two were by my side during a reading.

Then, one day they were gone. I tried to imagine them back but it didn't do any good. When I went in to guidance, I asked what happened. I was told they had merged with me, and we are now one. This showed me that we have power we aren't aware of, and we only have to learn to recognize it. Because of my fear, I was not letting these guides in. With them as part of me, I still have fear but the intensity is gone.

A couple of years down the line, I went to a doctor. He said something was wrong with my heart and sent me to a cardiologist to run some tests. I was scared to death.

While waiting for the appointment to get test results, I meditated. As I sat there, an angel started floating toward me—again this is in my imagination. She started to put her hand through my body where my heart is. In my thoughts I said, *Who are you?*

She answered, *I am your healer, and I am here to help*. She reached in, took my heart out, massaged it, and put it back. At that moment, I knew I would be all right. I went to the appointment to go over the tests. My doctor opened my chart and said all my tests were fine. His attitude was a little ho hum, but I knew what had happened and was thrilled.

We are not alone. All we have to do is allow our power.

• • •

A funny day. Talk about empowerment! Four or five women, were at my house, I can't remember why. They were women who had no power with their husbands whatsoever, and they were all upset.

I was trying to empower them but was getting frustrated and upset. I said, "Goddammit, one of you women say FUCK YOU!"

One said, "I can't even make myself spell it, Connie."

I said, "JUST SAY IT!!"

She tried, but she couldn't say it.

Meanwhile I am hollering, "Goddam son of a bitch. Goddam son of a bitch."

By the time they left they were yelling at each other, "Fuck you, you goddam son of a bitch." All of them! Laughing and swearing and having a great time. They were ready to fight. They had become their power!

Now, imagine the power it took to make this happen. Around 1941 or 42, a good seven years after my mother fled Oklahoma, she, my stepdad, and all of us kids were walking in Sacramento, down skid row, where farm workers gathered in friendship. Mom saw a man sitting on the sidewalk and said, "John? Is that you?" My half-brothers said, "Dad?" It was their father, my mother's first husband, sitting there drunk, and we happened to walk by. What are the odds? I don't remember much about the greeting, there was no hugging, no crying. He was filthy dirty. We brought him home, and he visited with the kids, took a bath, got himself fed and his clothes washed. The next day they drove him back to skid row and dropped him off. That was the last time the kids from Oklahoma saw their dad. I couldn't have imagined that my cruel stepfather would ever let this happen, but he did. Even as young as I was, I recognized my mom being quite emotionally affected by seeing him, I could feel the pain in her, and I think that she did love him. They had seven children and many years together. She was kind to him and had talked about going back to Oklahoma at some point; but we heard not too long after we saw him that he had died. The chances of crossing paths with him on the street were unimaginable, and I know it was no coincidence. It was a lesson in compassion.

The definition of power has changed over time for me. Power to my understanding was about people controlling people. Now, power is about being in control of myself. The difference is huge. Let's say that in the past, controlling my environment, the kids, Ray, and even friends, is what made me feel comfortable. Among family, nobody could do anything as well as I did. The holidays found me doing all the cooking because God knows nobody could smash those potatoes as well as I could. So, I ended up doing all the work. Nowadays that word *control* is about going with the flow and supervising my own heart. I am in charge of *me* now, not trying to manhandle those around me, although I still work at taking control from outside of myself and putting it inside myself. As long as control is inside myself, I can allow you to be who you are. But if I can't allow you to be who you are, then I am not in charge of myself. We must learn to know ourselves and not let other's perceptions of us cloud it.

I remember this woman coming to see me for a reading. She was a black minister at an all-black church. She said that the elders of her church hated the fact that she was going with a white man. This woman was engaging and funny, and I would have loved to attend her church just to hear her speak.

She called me one day saying," I have to tell you it really works!!"

Once I counsel someone, I don't retain the content, so I couldn't remember what I told her in our reading.

She continued, "My stupid white man came to the church meeting wanting to serve Kool-Aid to everyone. He disrupted everyone so he could serve Kool-Aid. I started to tell him to get the hell out of here, I have a meeting going on. But I heard your voice saying, 'SHUT UP, just shut up.' So, I didn't say anything. He took no more than ten minutes, served up his Kool Aid and felt like he was a part of the meeting and then left. Thank you. All I had to do was just allow him and not control him, and it worked out perfectly."

With one phone call, she taught me that sometimes we should just let life happen.

If I am holding painful or angry stuff inside, I have to bring it out. Being mealy-mouthed is the same as holding it all in. Maybe I NEED to say, "Screw you, you son of a bitch!" in order to be in peace. But we can't be angry and peaceful at the same time. The anger must be released first. This the difference between being controlling or being in control. Controlling behaviors are evidence of holding anger in.

In Tiburon, a town on the San Francisco Bay about fifty minutes from Benicia, I attended a gathering for the Buddhist teacher Lama Tharchin Rinpoche. People in Tiburon are wealthy, and they regularly sponsor speakers. This event was full and people were laying out tea, cheese, crackers and wine. Guests were helping themselves and visiting with each other. Then, in walks this little Buddhist man with his little Buddhist hat. He quietly sat at the table that was set for him, and I watched. As people came in, they brought him gifts of fruit, candy, and bread, which they placed on his table. All he did was to sit and smile pleasantly—and he did so all evening. By the time he started to speak, the table was covered with gifts. He spoke, but because of a hearing problem, I couldn't understand a word he said. I couldn't understand his accent.

On the way home, I asked Guidance what I was supposed to have learned. Hearing issue aside, I didn't know what the trip was even about. What was shown to me is that when we are peaceful, we are open to receiving. His table was full, the rest of our tables were empty. We were getting our own food and trying to chit chat while this little man sat and smiled as his table grew full. I thought Oh My God, all I have to do in this life is remain peaceful and the gifts appear. Our gifts reside in our inner peace, but it is the hardest thing ever to remain peaceful. It is about going beyond our reality, our experience, and seeing truth.

Because of the learning and reading disability I mentioned, I've had a hard time with book learning. Perhaps that is why I came to see life as a series of lessons of the spirit rather than training the brain. Regardless, angels have arrived when I needed help learning. Louella Madson was one of those angels. Without her I never would have finished eleventh grade. She was brilliant, and ended up valedictorian of the class. She came from a very poor family and was molested when she was about eleven years old. The child molester wasn't caught until he tried to get me into his car. I was on the way home from school one day, was also around eleven years old, and he pulled up alongside as I walked. He leaned through the open car window with fifty dollars in his hand, saying he would give it to me if I let him take me home. That was a fortune to most of us at the time, but he scared me, so I ran home, immediately telling my mom. We went right back to school to warn about this guy, but the principal already knew. I had seen two men hanging around the school. I thought they were old codgers with nothing to do. I found out later they were detectives trying to catch this creep. I was the first one they talked to because I was the one who blew the whistle. I told my story, and it turned out that many others had a story about this molester. too. He had molested several girls at our school, and my best friend Louella was one of them. I asked her why she never told me, and she said she was afraid because he had said he would kill her friends if she told. This was her first sexual experience. Her parents were religious, and she had terrible guilt over it.

Louella ended up prostituting. When I was about eighteen, she was working in Reno. She had a pimp, but I didn't know how that worked. This was the late fifties. Interestingly, she felt sorry for me because I was so poor. She drove a Cadillac and wore fur coats. She breezed into to my shop for a haircut when she was home for a visit and ordered the most expensive color and perm. She brought me "trick" dresses. This is a dress with a hook that you could just flip and the dress would fall off or you could close the hook on if you wanted to dress quickly. She wanted to dress me up because I didn't have many clothes. When I asked her what the dresses were for, she said, "Sometimes we have to get in and out of our clothes fast." In those days the police were after them. She said, "Sometimes we have to jump out the window." She would bring fur coats just so we could dress up together and drive around in her convertible. It was great fun.

One day, my boss said to me, "What did you say your friend does for a living?"

I thought quickly and said, "Oh she sells jewelry." I couldn't think of anything else.

Louella married one of her johns. By this time her pimp was hooked on heroin and was beating the hell out of her, so she got out of the business and married a one-legged truck driver who was good to her. If I ever got pregnant, I was to let her know; she could help. At this time, only prostitutes could get an abortion. Otherwise, she was careful about what she told me—for example she never told me her trick name—for my protection. If anyone ever came to talk to me about her, I wouldn't recognize the name. One of the most exciting days of my life was when she took me to meet her pimp. A small, skinny Mexican man, he fulfilled the stereotype with greasy hair and a sneaky, thin mustache. Later, I wondered how such a little guy could hold such power over her. Here I was, naive and young, having only heard about whores from people who were passing judgment on them. I remember saying, 'Louella, you're a prostitute? Really? My friend is a prostitute?" To me this was exciting, exotic. I was sort of proud of her.

For my part, I never judged her choices. She was the sweetest and truest best friend. During one of our visits in Reno, she told me about the molestation and the unrelenting guilt she felt. She said she started going downhill after that. Maybe that caused her to look at prostitution as a way of life. Later, she suffered through an abortion and again her guilt was heavy.

Life moved on. We both married. Every now and then we talked, but not too often. The last year of her life, she called me three times, trying to get us together, but I was always busy. The last time she called, she happened to be in the area. I was "too busy" once again. Now, I think, why didn't I just take time to see her? Not too long after that she died of a heart attack—way too young, only in her fifties. She might have felt her time was short. I could have changed an appointment and made space for her. I didn't learn my lesson with Donald. Apparently, I had to learn it again. We always have a choice, and power comes in choosing wisely.

• • •

My friend, Cookie, died of pancreatic cancer. She was someone who lived to please people. I went to see her a few days before she died. She was in bed, so frail and so skinny. All I could see were these big eyes. What did she want to know? "Connie, can I make you some coffee?"

On my way home I went in to my inner voice and asked Guidance why I lost my two best friends at such an early age. I was told, "You no longer have to feel guilty and you no longer have to please." When someone dies, they represent something you need to let go of. Luella represented a life of guilt, and Cookie had what Oprah calls "the disease to please."

Life is such an illusion. I would like to drum that into everyone. It is all in the perception, our way of interpreting or understanding something. Choose to stay in the flow, feel the peace. I think I have to work my ass off to make a certain amount of money in order to survive, but I'm just part of the sideshow I created. Once you put yourself in the flow of peace, what matters is right there, waiting for you to trust how the Universe works.

I've gotten everything I ever wanted. Not one thing is left on the list that I wanted but haven't gotten. I was cleaning our toilet one day when it hit home. It was one of TWO toilets inside our house! I was on my hands and knees, cleaning this toilet, and I started laughing. When I was a kid working in those fields, watching those nice cars roll by, I told myself, "I want a car. I want a house. I want a telephone, an indoor toilet, and in order to have them, I want a white man." I was laughing because I had been bitching about cleaning the damned toilet when there I was with everything I ever wanted.

A client came in for a haircut and a reading. I was working from home. This woman said, "Oh Connie, I would just die if I could have a home like yours!"

I thought, "Really?"

My second client of the day came in, saying, "Have you seen the homes in Southampton? I would die for one of those homes."

Third client showed up and said, "Have you been over to Blackhawk . . ." And *she* lived in Southampton!

Wow, three in one day, what was going on here? I asked Guidance and was told that all is illusion. Each person has a perspective based on experience, their value system, original culture, etc. Two people can look at the same situation and see it two completely different ways. I view from my inner space of being poor most of my early life. I thought I needed a house first, based on having been the daughter of farm laborers and moving from place to place. I wanted security in the form of owning a home. None of these women came from a background of poverty. They imagined they could thrive and be happy if they had an en suite master bathroom with a Jacuzzi. I was thrilled with indoor plumbing that flushed. It's all relative.

When you don't know who you are, you feel like there's a space you're trying to fill. Like you're trying to play cards with half a deck. But material things don't make you happy. Really, the only way you can feel whole is to stay in the peaceful flow of who you are. I often get complaints from women who are on a spiritual path and who say they *need* their husbands to understand their quest, that they feel a *need* to share it with them. I need. I need. I need. But then I take a look: if this spiritual journey is so important to us women, why aren't we sharing it with our partners? Why aren't they part of it?

Ray's view on spirituality was that it's pretty silly. I wanted him to accept me, but why was I not accepting him? I *needed* to let it be, and to go with the flow. If I could not accept him, or you, or anyone for who they are, I could not and cannot be peaceful.

I was talking to a young woman one day. She was so upset. She said, "Connie I get so irritated with my father, he just doesn't understand anything spiritual. He makes fun of me."

Now, I know her dad, and he is one of the most generous and kind people. He would give her his soul. But he doesn't happen to agree with her philosophy. She wanted him to be spiritual along with her but also for his own sake, to give him the gift of finding inner peace.

I said to her, "Christine, your father is one of the most spiritual people I know. He is kind, loving. He would die for you. He would give you anything. I bet if I were to call him right now needing a loan, he would give it to me. That's pretty spiritual."

I told her I thought she wasn't really looking at what a spiritual reality truly is.

"You are looking at words," I said. "He just puts different words to it than you do." Her father was intellectual, and that could be confused with being cold, which he was not. It was only the disparity in philosophy and vocabulary. Again, it is going with the flow, accepting others for who they are, so you can be in peace.

When Christine was fourteen, her family went on a ski trip and rented snowmobiles. Hers went off the side of the trail, and she almost died. A caring, loving doctor saved her. Christine saw her future in him. When I saw her next, she had decided to become a doctor. The experience changed her idea of what she wanted to be in her life. She set up her intention. She vibrated her intention to become a doctor, and you might remember that the universe hears only our vibration. If she were to shift into doubt or fear, she would have created an equally powerful flow in the opposite direction.

By comparison, I decided in my mind that in order to get out of working in the fields, I needed a white man, so, I created it. I wanted to be a hairdresser. I decided to create that when I was six years old. The idea stirred in me as I watched my aunt put on make-up. She came over to paint herself and do her hair. I watched her, fascinated, knowing I wanted to be a beautician.

I also knew then that I wanted a house, a car, and a toilet. I imagined it, and it happened.

I could never understand the saying, "It's just your imagination." Imagination is everything. Get into the peaceful flow, become an observer, and set it free.

The ability to manifest is part of your power. Put your desire out to the Universe in your thoughts and let go without expectation. But you *must* let go in order to manifest what you want.

When my friend got a new Lexus, she picked me up and took me for a ride. I thought, "OH MY GOD, I want a Lexus!"

Then, I didn't think about it anymore.

A few days later, I went to the bank, and as I was parking my car a young man backing out rammed my car. Suddenly, I had no car, and in my reality, I couldn't afford to run down and buy a Lexus. I called my good friend who owned a Toyota dealership. I said if you can give me a good deal on a Toyota, I will come and see you today.

He said, "Connie, I don't sell Toyotas anymore. I have a Lexus dealership."

I said, "Oh, I can't afford a Lexus, Mickey." As I had forgotten about sending that original desire out to the Universe, I didn't fear not having a Lexus and gave no thought to "can or can't have it." Since my desire came with no expectations, it was easy to manifest. Once we involve ourselves in the sideshows of expectations or judgments (such as "I can't afford it," or feeling mad that we aren't making enough money), we get out of flow and cloud our message to the Universe.

Expectations are our greatest source of suffering, because no matter whether a thing meets your expectation or not, that thing can be taken away from you. That's spiritual law. When Deborah was growing up, I always wanted what was "best for Deborah." This means that my expectation was that she would marry a white man, so she, too, could be successful.

As you know, every one of her boyfriends was dark. First was a little alcoholic Mexican boy about sixteen. Next was a black boy, and then she married a man from the Middle East.

Expectation and judgment remove us from flow—flow being my description of the place of peacefulness. Expectation creates dissatisfaction. Judgment is where karma is received. I can't emphasize that enough. Intentions, smiles, hugs, laughter, joy, kindness, music, exercise, meditation, healthy food, sleep, heartfelt sharing, enjoying nature, and living in gratitude, all keep our vibrations high, which helps us remain peaceful and manifest desires. As long as we keep body and spirit separate, we will never be happy because we will always feel a little bit empty. Most of the people I have done readings for are walking around empty, and they have reached the point in their lives where they are questioning life and its purpose. They have done everything, have everything, but still are not happy. They are separated from spirit, living only in the body, lost in physical existence. The body was given to us because of what we have to learn from physical experiences and sensations, so that we might grow toward spirit. Without a body, without the senses, we couldn't learn—it's the body that allows us to feel.

A HEART MUST BE BROKEN IN ORDER TO OPEN

On November 17, 2008, a hammer came down, and the shape of my world changed forever.

I lost my beautiful Deborah to cancer.

Losing Deborah took me to a new level of consciousness, a level of awakening I'd never have achieved without the loss. My heart had to be crushed to get there. A horrible price to pay.

One day I was sobbing and asking why I had to lose her. Did I choose this experience? If so, how the hell could I have done this to myself? Guidance came in to tell me, *Sometimes, a heart has to be broken in order to open.* I never realized that I had been walking this earth with a closed heart. But I could feel it: a closed heart feels like resistance, holding back. I have always been full of compassion, love, and understanding, but I didn't love unconditionally. I loved carefully. For instance, I could love you if you loved me. But now, with an open heart, I can love you whether you love me or not. I can love people even if they are being difficult.

Now, I am able to see that we can't experience our journey and feel love and the vibration of love if we have a closed heart. You know the saying, "Dance as if there is nobody watching?" Well, I needed to learn to love as if nobody is judging. Even the smallest lessons can take a lifetime to learn. Evidently, I needed a sledge hammer. I realize now that my purpose is to share this and other stories so that you, my readers, can take from them whatever it is you need.

Since Deborah's passing, I have learned to see other people as absolute perfection, just as, in my eyes, she was perfection. She was fair and considerate, didn't judge or hold grudges. Instead, she told off a person elegantly, proved her point, and moved on. Her students respected her because she cared enough to take the time to understand them and always went to bat for them. Some caused trouble, still, she could see through their pain and find goodness. Her kindness showed in her eyes, snapping to attention if anyone needed her support. She used to say she had "very little baggage, just a carry-on."

Deborah loved animals. Her big brown, mixed-breed, mostly-Labrador dog, Patty, was by her side as she lay dying. I felt horrible when I tried to take Patty outside to do her business. She did not want to leave Deborah's side. She pulled on the leash and cried, trying to get back in the house. Once inside, she ran straight to the side of the bed. I like to think that she and Patty are together now.

Deborah showed me I need to focus on what is important and who is around me, not just what I want to do at the moment. Years ago, when I was doing hair, I was mixing tint in the back of the salon. One of the other girls was back there and said, "Connie, you are like a goddamn bull in a china shop. You walk back here and you knock everybody out of the way, and you aren't even aware we are in your way."

I had to admit she was right. I had been that way my whole life—focused on what I was doing and the hell with anyone else. Now I am learning to slow down and remember what is important. This is what losing my Deborah has done for me.

Love always has been a hard word. For me, it had no meaning. My mother never told us she loved us, nor was she outwardly affectionate. She showed her love by providing. I don't know that I ever told my mother I loved her. When she was in her early sixties, she stopped working in the fields. She was in pretty good shape until age seventy-five, when her health started failing. Despite the stress, she remained physically active. Since she never learned to drive well, the family took her to appointments and activities. Occasionally, I resented the use of my time for this. I couldn't see that I was missing the opportunity to connect with her. She lived to be eighty-three. When I look back. I see the lessons: forgiveness, love, compassion, and non-judgment. She never hugged or kissed us but she taught by example, just by being who she was.

Ray's ex-wife constantly told their daughters she loved them, but emotionally she abused them. I got pissed when, within minutes of us walking into our house with the girls the phone would ring, and it would be their mother, and she would want to talk to the kids. We would hear, "Okay Mom, I love you." Then they would get off the phone and sadly say, "Dad, could we go home?" How could creating guilt in a child be love? Now, I can look back and recognize her feelings of loss and abandonment. She was hurting, too, and hurting those kids because of it. Could I have helped her find her truth? I regret that I didn't even think to try.

Most of us walk with a shield around us for much of our lives. Childhood wounds caused us to create those shields, as protection: denial, rejection, shyness, etc. Mostly, we are not raised to have an open heart, rather we are raised to be careful. When we speak carefully to our family and friends, we tend to choose our words cautiously instead of saying what we feel. Remember the dream where I was on stage, and I was supposed to figure out what my act was? When we change our speech to pacify others, we are adopting other people's stage act as our own. I want you to know it is time to recognize the act *you* have created—and live it.

I no longer feel there is anything about me I need to protect. In that way, I feel free. I can say "I love you" and really mean it, without fear of getting hurt. I am more peaceful than I have ever been. The pain of loss never goes away—that will be with me forever. Because that loss brought me greater understanding, I have a level of inner peace I didn't have before. That doesn't mean I walk around with this understanding, it just means that when something happens, I realize that all is my illusion and ask myself what the lesson is. I look at what's happened and realize again and again that the lesson never stops presenting itself until we truly learn it. When you lose the love of your life and you know that person is irreplaceable, you can either go down into despair or go into your inner self and ask why it happened. Then you grow with it. The inner peace I feel comes from knowing that I am only here for a short time. Deborah came into my life as my teacher, and she was a huge part of my journey. The only thing that saves me and keeps me at an even emotional level of peace is knowing I have purpose and the need to share that purpose. That doesn't mean I have to teach it, but I have to model it by loving unconditionally.

• • •

About a week or so after my mom passed, my phone rang. When I answered, my mom, who had a very distinctive voice said, "Connie."

I said "MOM," and she said "Connie" two more times very clearly.

I never told anyone about this because it was too weird, and I thought nobody was ever going to believe me. So, I forgot about it.

Then, after we moved to Benicia, a well-known psychic friend of mine came to me for a reading. Her best friend had just died, and she wanted to connect. She told me people who have passed CAN come through the phone. I was flattened! I told her that my mom had come through to me on the phone and that I had never told anyone. She said it happens all the time.

A friend called me one evening, crying uncontrollably. Her beloved little dog had died. Ray was sitting next to me and heard both sides of the conversation. She was hard to understand, and he asked why she was crying so hard. I told him the little dog had died from an infected tooth. My friend was completely distraught. I felt bad for her, and a couple of days later I called to see how she was doing.

She said she had not called me!

Thank God Ray had heard the call, too, or I would have thought I'd gone nuts. Evidently the dog was living and well. I told her about the infected tooth and she was concerned enough to take the dog to the vet. Sure enough, a tooth needed to be removed before the infection spread and killed her. Divine intervention saved the dog.

The greatest gift I received during my time of grief were two messages Deborah left on my answering machine. In one case she was sighing. It was her familiar sigh, which Ray and I both clearly recognized. The other one was her voice, truly her voice, saying, "I'm not sure. I think I did not die." I feel it was because of my belief system that I received those messages. When you suffer a great loss, you must develop a belief system—any system that helps give you peace. I have to believe Deborah's death made me a better person, that now I have better tools to help people, and most of all that she is still with me in spirit and that one day we will be reunited. Deborah's ashes are with me because I draw comfort from feeling her nearness. A woman friend, an excellent channel, told me that Deborah is with me because she knows I'm afraid to be alone.

Nobody really knows what's on the other side. People who've survived near-death experiences all have different stories. What I know, and I find comfort in this, is that I am a life-long student, and I believe that I am only here to learn. And I believe that we are here to share with others as we grow at different levels.

A woman in one of my classes called to say she wouldn't return because I hadn't given her any attention. In the past, I might have tried to make it all right. I would have called to say I was sorry she felt that way and tried to make it better—I would try to "fix" it. But now I won't participate in that as I realize the situation is not about me. Instead, I would stand back and allow her to have that feeling. I am not going to try to change the feeling, since she needs what she will learn from working through it. If she were to figure it out and decided to return to talk with me, I would welcome her with open arms.

Whatever our issues are, they are part of us, always. As we recognize the issues and learn to handle them, such as abandonment or rejection, we can work on these things within ourselves. As we gradually learn the lesson, we are bothered by it less and less. If you and I were having a conversation ten years ago during which you said you didn't like my hair, I would have taken it personally. I would have felt rejected and disliked. Now that my perception has shifted, I can realize that you have a right to your own opinion and that your opinions are none of my business.

I may be perfect just as I am, but it has taken me over sixty years to own that. Because my heart was not taken care of as a child and because of what I witnessed from the womb, I came to this lifetime feeling unwanted. I lacked the necessary acknowledgement from my mother and lost my birth father for a time, and so I closed my heart. I pretended to be okay and protected myself by sharing only what I thought people would accept as perfection. The panic attacks represented the part of me that needed to share what I knew with other people—a whole new "me" was trying to be born. The Universe knew what I needed, and so did my body, but I didn't.

Similarly, my two loving stepdaughters were given to me because the Universe knew I would lose my Deborah. I don't know what I would have done without those two girls, but when they first came into my life, I resisted getting close to them. I was twenty years old, and hell, I didn't want to be a parent, I only wanted Ray. I didn't want to raise his kids. I even thought that they were jealous of me, but in reality, I was the jealous one. I see now they were put on my path to save my life, to be there for me. I see the karma. I was a stepdaughter who learned to hate, then became a stepmother who learned to love. Pam and Mary are in their fifties now and are the same people they were as kids, two of the most loving people I have known. I think as parents, we miss that sometimes. We see the rooms they don't clean, the right clothes they don't choose, or the homework they don't do. It took the death of Deborah for me to see *oh my God, those are two of the sweetest, most loveable girls I have ever met.* I have such regret over this.

When Pam and Mary were three and five years old, we were granted custody because their birth mother was making terrible choices, and ours was a stable home. As Mary describes it, "Mom was flighty and always sticking up for her latest man. We were too afraid to speak up."

After about a year, and promises of better parenting, the girls went back to live with her. In seventh grade, Mary asked to come back and stayed with us for about a year. But she missed her sister, Pam, and by then younger siblings were in the picture, so Mary decided to move back with her mother. When Mary was in high school, Ray's ex started running wild again, and Mary was being neglected. He couldn't bear it, so he brought her home. She lived with us until she started college. Mary now says, "I wouldn't have graduated had you not intervened." Deborah, Pam, and Mary were all well aware of my psychic abilities. Mary laughs, "Being a teenager with psychic stepmother—I couldn't get away with anything!" Meanwhile, Deborah, true to form, made sure they were full-fledged sisters, sharing a room, sharing secrets, stories, and love.

Pam once said to a friend of mine, "I cannot remember a time before Connie. In many ways, she was a mother to me. Growing up with her was interesting. We elevated tables. She read Tarot cards for me, regressed me through prior lives, and introduced me to many incredible people along the way. I have been able to attend many of her classes. I feel like my life has been so blessed, and when I have needed someone to listen or a shoulder to cry on, she has always been there for me. Being a part of Connie's family has always been fun! Her dad, our Grandpa Cherry, was a real character with a great sense of humor. He was always singing and dancing. It was a big, loving family, and every get-together was a huge event with lots of great food and laughs. I love them all very much. Deborah Lee Jackson was and will forever be my baby sister. Her smile was like sunshine, and she had a ready laugh. She was always so caring to everyone who knew her—an inspiration to our family, her students, and friends. She was brave facing breast cancer and never lost her charming personality. She loved everyone she knew and was a great sister, mother, daughter, and friend. I love and miss her every day."

Deborah was four years younger than Mary and six years younger than Pam. In her short forty-eight years, Deborah married, gave birth to a daughter, and became a teacher and school counselor. She was so beloved by her students and colleagues that the final weekend of her life proved to be one of the most loving events I have ever witnessed. Deborah's daughter, Josie, Ray, and I decided to open the doors to visitors. Though she wasn't able to talk much, she saw between two hundred fifty and three hundred current and former students, colleagues, family, and friends who came by her house to say goodbye. We knew they needed to see her, and she needed to see them and feel this love. The house was filled with flowers, food, and tears.

As the end of his life was nearing, Ray and I were together in our living room. He was lying on the rented hospital bed in front of the picture window with a view of our peaceful backyard that hosted assorted birds and squirrels. He mostly slept at this point and could no longer enjoy the sight he always loved. I was sitting close by, lost in thought, when he suddenly held his arms up as though reaching to the sky and said, "Deborah." A few hours later, he was gone. I am comforted to know she was there to help him through his transition. It was so like her.

• • •

The product of regret is the opposite of peace, and I have suffered regret most of my life.

My older sister Ruth was a kind person and my personal savior. When my mom got after me, Ruth soothed me by babying me. Like Yin to my Yang, Ruth was there for me. Years later, as an adult, I was holding a workshop in San Diego. Food was ordered, reservations made, and the bill paid. Dr. Siri, now deceased, was an amazing healer from Sri Lanka who later emigrated to the Sacramento area. He was going to demonstrate healing methods, and my session was to be about how to hear our inner voice. I was meeting him at the airport to drive him in.

At about nine o'clock the night before, my niece called and said, "If you want to see your sister, you better come, she is dying." We went to Stockton and were there maybe an hour or so. I said, "Ruth, I have to go to San Diego, but I will be back as soon as I can."

Ruth whispered faintly, "Connie, don't leave me." But I did. I left the hospital, knowing she was going to die, knowing this was the end of my dear sister, but I went into denial because I didn't know what else to do. I had no way to reach Dr. Siri, and he needed to be picked up at the airport. I felt caught between two forces. I went to San Diego and did the first day of a two-day workshop. Then Deborah called to tell me, "Aunt Ruth died."

And then, the worst.

When my Deborah was fighting for her life, she called me saying, "Mom, are you coming over tonight to give me energy?"

We had a standing date that I would come over Monday nights, but I was feeling bone tired that evening and said, "Honey, I am so tired tonight. Can I just send you some energy from here, and I will see you tomorrow?"

Again, she said, "Couldn't you just come tonight?" I said I couldn't go. By the next morning, she was almost comatose and never improved. Goddammit, every time someone I love needs me, I am not there.

Overcome by grief, I sat crying one day over my regrets and my inner voice said, *you can never go back, but you can correct it now*. I knew exactly what that meant. I had Pam and Mary, my stepdaughters, and I could love them and make it right. In spiritual reality, time doesn't exist, everything is right now. Wanting to go back is natural, and a redo is not possible, but things can be redone in the present. Deborah, Pam, and Mary are all spiritual beings, alive or dead. I can be a loving person now to everybody in my reality and replace those past mistakes. We are energy, and nothing more. This was new information to me, and I didn't receive it until after Deborah's death. I had to keep learning and sharing or I couldn't endure the pain. I went to a healer during this time of growth and reflection, and the night after our session had a dream that golden seeds, seeds of love and compassion, were spewing out of my heart. I knew it meant that I was a seed planter and that I must plant.

Deborah was a seed planter. Years ago, when she moved to Benicia and took a teaching job, she made many friends. She loved her job and the people whose lives she touched loved her. Deborah was not the least bit interested in anything spiritual. She stayed on the fringes but brought people in to me. Once, she asked if she could bring some of her school colleagues and friends for a small, free workshop. It was fun, and they were supportive, interested learners. One of her friends came to me saying that she was grateful to Deborah because she had opened a whole new world for her. Another came to tell me that that because of my daughter, she had become spiritual. After Deborah passed, one of these women called to ask me to do a workshop at her house. She had about fifteen women attend, and I did an all-day program. Next, she asked if I would do a meditation group once a month. Of course! These women were picking up where Deborah left off and brought a community together.

I think about karma. I have mentioned how I snapped at my mom for talking too much about my run-away sister Ruby. I had no patience when it came to Ruby, but when I lost Deborah, that was my first thought, and boy did I ever have to walk that karma. Mom had lost two kids in Oklahoma to disease and then Ruby. I never realized what that pain must have been like. I think it is important to see how we are creating karma, that we pay attention to lessons and that we realize that we can never know it all. This lifetime is a journey without end. When I was young, I thought I knew what it would take to make me peaceful, but I am still figuring that out at my advanced age. I think that a lifetime isn't so much about finding answers but more about creating questions. Isn't that what growth is all about?

Mind/body connection, which we've already discussed, became personal for me after Deborah's passing. My last surgery was totally connected to her. For years, my doctor had been saying I needed a colonoscopy. I said, "No way do I want anybody going up my ____. NO!

But then things got to the point that every time I ate, I became nauseated. My doctor ran several tests, yet couldn't find anything wrong. Let me tell you, when you walk around nauseated for a year, it starts to wear on you. When I finally went back to the doctor, she went over all of my tests and said, "Connie, you must have a colonoscopy."

At this point, I agreed and so the test was done. Two polyps were removed and a third was unreachable. I was sent to a surgeon. I said to the surgeon, "I am seventy-four years old, so there has to be a really good reason to have this surgery."

He said, "Chemo."

I said, "OK."

During the surgery he actually removed four polyps and afterward he said he thought it was meant to be as the polyps were pre-cancerous. I remember thinking that losing Deborah was a feeling like being kicked in my gut. I had continued to hold the emotional pain there. Trapping feelings and not sharing them appropriately creates blocks in the chakras, the centers of power in the human body. These blocks can create illness. I think of the saying that there are people who get cancer and people who give cancer.

An umbilical cord is a life source during that time when a child is wholly dependent. When it is cut, independent growth for both child and mother is initiated. To me, the cord is the symbol of the fact that children are extensions of their parents. It's no wonder the people we love have such power in our lives.

When I was a child, I would gaze up past the clouds and into the blue and wonder if I could cut open the sky, what would be on the other side? I am still that child, looking for the answers to life's questions. Ironically, now my one remaining question is—do any of us have the answers? I think that my collection of knowledge is just the tip of the iceberg. There is much more to know. Each time I reached a different perspective and acquired more wisdom, I thought, *Oh, that's the answer!* Then something else would happen to bring about more growth in me and I would once again think I had all the answers. Really, wisdom grows and intensifies the more we take in and the more lessons we come to understand. Until our last breath, our one constant is change, which means school never ends. It is the platform on which we are born with its series of classrooms, the goal of which is not to teach us to endure or to persevere, although those are useful strategies for living, but to awaken us to the purity and the wholeness of love.

The characters, the loves, the friendships, enemies, and acquaintances—these form the sum of my life. *People* have been my teachers, my guides, and my angels. Many have wanted to write my story, but I wasn't ready until now. I feel that I am at a spiritual level where I can share without holding back. When I look over my life, I wouldn't change being poor nor would I exchange any of my experiences along the way. I know we learn by comparison, and I had the best examples of this: sweet birth dad vs. mean stepfather, nurturing sister Ruth vs. no-nonsense mom. These comparative lessons fostered my growth. It all comes together when I recognize the patterns. Everyone, especially those I love, have been teaching me about me.

MESSAGE FROM CONNIE

In meditating during the writing of this book, these messages came to me at different times directly from Source:

We all are designed to be compassionate, just as we are designed to breathe. Compassion goes beyond the heart or the mind. Compassion is the receiving of Source energy and the expression of the essence of that energy. When you are aware of Source flowing through you, compassion follows naturally, with ease and eagerness. This cannot be forced as it is not something you create, but it can be resisted, and if you resist Source within yourself and do not acknowledge the pure energy that creates every facet of your life and being, you cannot easily access that within yourself which allows compassion to flow.

A part of yourself always remembers that life is a game to be played with excitement and awareness. There are roles you play in life and roles are part of the game. It is right to play these roles and lose yourself at times in the playing of these roles, but you are more than these roles. The role you play is not the "real" you. It is in many ways a character, an act. If you identify with the role, it is not easy to identify with the person you really are.

The truth of the self cannot be seen if not looked for. It cannot be heard if not listened to. For a long time, people have searched for a single "truth" outside of themselves, but the truth is within each person and each person has their own. There is much to be heard in the quiet of a peaceful mind. Passions are flaring at this time in your world and personalities are showing themselves like never before. People are learning to honor their individual voices and yet few are listening to the peacefulness within them. So many want what they will not allow. They do not yet realize that what they are wanting to see in the world, they must allow themselves to experience within. They want peace but do not feel peaceful. They want wealth but do not feel worthy of it. They want joy but will not allow themselves to feel joyful about who and where they are, so all of their wants exist in a future that has no way of arriving because they are not allowing the present to contain their desires. It takes practice. We do not say that it is easy at first to make the transition from a lifetime of practicing one way into a new life of practicing in another way. But we will say it gets easier the more you allow yourself, first to want it, and then to practice it. You honor your desires by allowing yourself to feel love for yourself, when you do that, your light is on. Everyone has the knowledge within themselves about what they truly want. They will deny this if there is fear attached to desire, but it does not mean they do not know. Source does not resist you at any time but you as an extension of Source focused in the physical world, do have the option of resisting. It is part of the human design, the game of physical life for people. You are in essence creatures of choice. The choice is always available and the choice is always necessary. People can get very confused and yet in that confusion they can find clarity. So, make clarity the goal. Make loving yourself the goal. Having the choice is what makes doing it an accomplishment. If you didn't have the choice, there would be no point to this life.

Tools to help you practice love, find inner peace, and to understand the difference between living and being alive in Source.

QUOTES TO PONDER

- From Deepak Chopra: "God is the evolutionary impulse of the universe. God is infinite creativity, infinite love, infinite compassion, and infinite caring."

- From Wayne Dyer: "God is the highest place within each and every one of us. It is our divine self."

- From Eckhart Tolle: "God is beyond all the forms of life, but also in it dwells every form of life as their essence. God is both beyond and within."

- From Mastin Kipp: "God is Love."

- From Gary Zukav: "God is layers upon layers of compassion and wisdom way beyond ours."

Goals for the Spiritual Life:

Instead of Fear:Aim for Love:
(Human self/student)(Higher self/teacher)
Drama/Solution
Victim/Acceptance
Struggle/Allow
Resistance/Receiving
Judgment/Non-judgment
Rejection/Trust
Distrust/Sharing
Guilt/Unconditional
Attach/Detach
Jealous/Grateful
Denial/Generous
Anger/Kindness

NUMBERS AND WHAT THEY REPRESENT

1. New Beginnings (beginning a new life cycle)
2. Balance (spiritual with physical)
3. Body Mind Spirit (awakening the harmony within the trinity)
4. Balancing (relationship energy)
5. Change
6. Guidance (reaching higher for wisdom)
7. Magic (can create)
8. Prosperity (infinity, flow of consciousness)
9. Completion (of a life cycle, moving on to the next)

For instance, add the numbers of your address and come up with one digit. If your address is 5864 and it adds up to 22, then add those digits and come up with 4—personal relationship with self. More information about color symbols is available in Betty Bethards books. (Please see Bibliography.)

MEDITATION GUIDE

Start by relaxing your body, taking deep breaths.

Be in the present moment, sitting with your body relaxed.

Follow your breath as it goes in and out. Let your body further relax. (Teaching people to meditate can be hard, because I tell them to relax but they don't know what that means.)

Start at your head, willing your head and neck muscles to release.

Visualize each body part on the way to your toes and will them to let go, be jelly.

Be present in the moment with your breath: hear it feel it, try to hear your heartbeat.

Get into your imagination. Don't control it, and see what comes to mind. If you have a meditation leader, and they suggest imagining you are at the ocean, look around see the sand, the people, and the dogs playing and running at the surf. Stay focused on what you can see, the sand, smell the salt water, feel the warm sun. Hear the shore birds and the waves hitting the beach and crawling up the sand. Be there and sense where your imagination takes you. Imagine yourself bathed in gold light beaming over you and surrounding you.

I like to silently, just in my mind, say to the Universe, *I ask the Divine light of love and compassion to fill and surround me, wisdom to flow through me, and guidance to guide me. I am blessed, I am blessed, I am blessed.*

Now, let that settle, breathe, and allow your imagination to get you in focus. Sometimes simply by going into your imagination, a happy place, you will feel peaceful. If your mind wants to take you to the mountain top, go there as long as it is a peaceful place. As soon as you get out of that peaceful place, the stress seeps in. It is like being in the eye of a hurricane. As long as you are in the eye you are peaceful and safe—as soon as you slip out of the eye you are thrown around. That's what life does to us.

Your mind doesn't stay put. You can actually be meditating and not realize it. If your mind wanders, bring it back to the quiet place. Now you are actually meditating.

The absolute best is when you get totally lost to the point that you are taking a journey. You don't know what is coming next. When you come back from the meditative state take notes and see what you learned. Look at the symbols, and know you can create a relaxed state when you need to in the midst of your hectic world.

QUESTIONS AND CONTEMPLATIONS: A READER'S GUIDE:

- The Big Question—Where do you think our original energy comes from? I believe there is a force that is guiding us, but who or what?

- What is your fear?

- Is your family a circle of energy where everything is one?

- We are always evolving, is our soul evolving? Does our soul increase in wisdom in subsequent lives?

- Our thoughts power us. We constantly create, so we need to be clear about what we want to create.

- We go through many levels of awareness. As we awaken, the aperture of the lens we see through gets larger so we see can see our life's blessings.

- Our illusion is created through our experience. Nothing is one size fits all. It's relative based on our level of understanding.

- The person has to become more important than your expectations.

- "Illusion is perspective" said Abraham.

- Truth changes with wisdom all the time—allow it to evolve.

- Never feel trapped. We are always free to make choices.

- Focus on success, never lack.

- Get out of your own way, don't be limited by beliefs.

- Fear is an excellent teacher. It gets our attention.

- Judge the importance of things by how they relate to peacefulness.

- We have to experience lack to experience joy. We learn from opposites.

- Frustration and anger deplete our power.

- If you could be the spiritual person you aspire to be, how would that differ from who you already are?

- You and I are in different form, but we are one. What we see in another is only a reflection of ourselves whether it is likeable or not. We can't feel the like or dislike if it isn't inside us.

- Can you see your Karmic debt? The more we judge the more karma we acquire.

SUGGESTED RESOURCES

Arntz, Wm., Chase, B., Vincente, M. Producers and Directors, (2006), *What the Bleep Do I Know?* DVD, U.S.A. Samuel Goldwin Films.

Bethards, Betty (1992). *The Dream Book; Symbols for Self-Understanding*, Petaluma, CA: Inner Light Foundation.

Blom 10. "Are You an Indigo Child, Too?" *The Psychology of Extraordinary Beliefs*. The Ohio State University. https://u.osu.edu/vanzandt/2019/04/16/indigo-child-movement/. Sept. 30, 2020.

Chopra, Deepak (2004). *Synchrodestiny*, N.Y. Simon and Schuster

Dyer, Wayne (2007). *Change Your Thoughts, Change Your Life,* Carlsbad, Ca: Hay House, Inc.

Hay, Louise. *You Can Heal Your Life*

Hicks, Esther and Jerry (2004). *Ask and It Is Given (The teachings of Abraham),* Carlsbad, CA: Hay House Inc.

MacLaine, Shirley (1984). *Out on a Limb*, N.Y. Bantam Books

Millman, Dan (2006). *Way of the Peaceful Warrior*, California, H.J. Kramer

Schucman, Helen (1977). *A Course in Miracles*, Mill Valley CA: Foundation for Inner Peace.

Stern, Jess (1989). *Edgar Cayce, The Sleeping Prophet*, N.Y. Bantam Books

ACKNOWLEDGMENTS

A great story comes to life only with the support of a capable team. My appreciation is heartfelt, primarily for Connie Jackson, who lived her remarkable life with style and grace, then chose to share it with me. I am also grateful for the time and care Connie's daughters, Mary Jackson Cawley and Pamela Jackson Crea, gave to the project. My gratitude extends also to my former teaching colleague, first reader and kindly critic, Laura Darrah Calvert. Paula Coomer, my accomplished editor, was pivotal in the successful completion of this book, and I can't imagine writing another without her enjoyable partnership.

Ray Jackson will always have my deepest gratitude for his eager and thoughtful support of both Connie and me. We wish his lifetime could have been much longer.

IN MEMORIAM
Ray Jackson
Nov. 9, 1932-June 2, 2017
Husband, Father, and Master Teacher

Connie Castro Jackson
September 27, 1937 – December 5, 2020
Wife, Mother, Inspirational Woman

ABOUT THE AUTHOR

Corliss Corazza is a retired educator from Northern California and a close friend and student of the late Connie Castro Jackson. A believer in life-long learning, Ms. Corazza embraced the ideology of the metaphysical as a logical, creative —and therefore spiritual— approach to living. She resides in the Bay Area with her husband Dave, goldendoodle Sophia, and twin orange tabbies.

NOTE FROM THE AUTHOR

Word-of-mouth is crucial for any author to succeed. If you enjoyed *Cut Open the Sky*, please leave a review online—anywhere you are able. Even if it's just a sentence or two. It would make all the difference and would be very much appreciated.

Thanks!
Corliss Corazza

We hope you enjoyed reading this title from:

BLACK ROSE writing™

www.blackrosewriting.com

Subscribe to our mailing list – *The Rosevine* – and receive **FREE** books, daily deals, and stay current with news about upcoming releases and our hottest authors.
Scan the QR code below to sign up.

Already a subscriber? Please accept a sincere thank you for being a fan of Black Rose Writing authors.

View other Black Rose Writing titles at www.blackrosewriting.com/books and use promo code **PRINT** to receive a **20% discount** when purchasing.

www.ingramcontent.com/pod-product-compliance
Lightning Source LLC
Chambersburg PA
CBHW071241070526
44583CB00017B/2283